Ethan Marcotte

RESPONSIVE WEB DESIGN

SECOND EDITION

MORE FROM THE A BOOK APART LIBRARY

HTML5 for Web Designers
Jeremy Keith

CSS3 for Web Designers
Dan Cederholm

The Elements of Content Strategy
Erin Kissane

Designing for Emotion
Aarron Walter

Mobile First
Luke Wroblewski

Design Is a Job
Mike Monteiro

Content Strategy for Mobile
Karen McGrane

Just Enough Research
Erika Hall

Sass for Web Designers
Dan Cederholm

On Web Typography
Jason Santa Maria

You're My Favorite Client
Mike Monteiro

Responsible Responsive Design
Scott Jehl

Publisher: Jeffrey Zeldman
Designer: Jason Santa Maria
Managing Director: Katel LeDû
Technical Editor: Anna Debenham
Copyeditor: Sally Kerrigan
Compositor: Rob Weychert
Ebook Production: India Amos

Editor, first edition: Mandy Brown
Technical Editor, first edition: Dan Cederholm
Copyeditor, first edition: Krista Stevens
Compositor, first edition: Neil Egan

ISBN: 978-1-9375571-8-8

A Book Apart
New York, New York
http://abookapart.com

10 9 8 7 6 5 4 3 2 1

TABLE OF CONTENTS

FOREWORD

LANGUAGE HAS magical properties. The word "glamour"—which was originally a synonym for magic or spell-casting—has its origins in the word "grammar." Of all the capabilities of language, the act of naming is the most magical and powerful of all. The short history of web design has already shown us the transformative power of language. Jeffrey Zeldman gave us the term "web standards" to rally behind. Jesse James Garrett changed the nature of interaction on the web by minting the word "Ajax."

When Ethan Marcotte coined the term "responsive web design" he conjured up something special. The technologies existed already: fluid grids, flexible images, and media queries. But Ethan united these techniques under a single banner, and in so doing changed the way we think about web design.

Ethan has a way with words. He is, of course, the perfect person to write a book on responsive web design. But he has done one better than that: he has written *the* book on responsive web design.

If you're hoping for a collection of tricks and tips for adding a little bit of superficial flair to the websites that you build, then keep looking, my friend. This little beauty operates at a deeper level.

When you've finished reading this book (and that won't take very long) take note of how you approach your next project. It's possible that you won't even notice the mind-altering powers of Ethan's words, delivered, as they are, in his light-hearted, entertaining, sometimes downright hilarious style; but I guarantee that your work will benefit from the prestidigitation he is about to perform on your neural pathways.

Ethan Marcotte is a magician. Prepare to be spellbound.

—Jeremy Keith

INTRODUCTION

OH. HI. It's great to see you again.

In this latest edition of *Responsive Web Design,* you'll find a whole host of changes: updated figures, fixed links, and a *truckload* of little corrections.

But, ultimately, the three main ingredients of a responsive design—flexible grids, fluid images, and media queries—are as relevant today as they were when I first coined the phrase. So while the structure of the book hasn't changed that much, I think you'll agree there are a lot of significant edits throughout. In the years since this book was first published, designers, agencies, and large organizations alike have been producing stellar responsive designs, pushing the concept forward. At every relevant opportunity, I've included their work, writings, and research.

One thing hasn't changed, though. You see, when I wrote an article about something called responsive web design (http://bkaprt.com/rwd2/0/) a few years ago, I didn't think for a *second* I'd be lucky enough to write a book on the topic. (Much less write another edition of it.) In other words: I'm still very humbled by the attention the idea of responsive design has gotten. But I'm also thankful because, well, that attention's due to you. Thanks for asking such great questions over email, for the feedback on Twitter, for recommending the book to your friends, and for building such fantastic responsive sites. This new edition wouldn't have been possible without your help. Even if you're reading this book for the first time, your interest in responsive design helped make this edition possible.

Thank you so, so much for reading my book. As I said the last time around, I can't wait to see what you'll make with it.

—Ethan

PS: The line about the pirate hat has not been edited in any way, as it was contributed by my wife, who continues to be much funnier and smarter than I am.

1 OUR RESPONSIVE WEB

> *Something there is that doesn't love a wall..."*
> —ROBERT FROST, "MENDING WALL"

AS I BEGIN writing this book, I realize I can't guarantee you'll read these words on a printed page, holding a tiny paperback in your hands. Maybe you're sitting at your desk with an electronic copy of the book up on your screen. Perhaps you're on your morning commute, tapping through pages on your phone, or swiping along on a tablet. Or maybe you don't even see these words as I do: maybe your computer is simply reading this book aloud.

Ultimately, I know so little about you. I don't know how you're reading this. I can't.

Publishing has finally inherited one of the web's central characteristics: flexibility. Book designer and publisher Craig Mod believes that his industry is quickly entering a "post-artifact" phase (http://bkaprt.com/rwd2/1/), that the digital age is revising our definition of what constitutes a "book."

FIG 1.1: The canvas, even a blank one, provides a boundary for an artist's work. (Photo by Cara St.Hilaire: http://bkaprt.com/rwd2/2/)

Of course, web designers have been grappling with this for some time. In fact, our profession has never had an "artifact" of its own. At the end of the day, there isn't any *thing* produced by designing for the web, no tangible object to hold, to cherish, to pass along to our children. But despite the oh-so-ethereal nature of our work, the vocabulary we use to talk about it is anything but: "masthead," "whitespace," "leading," even the much-derided "fold." Each of those words is directly inherited from print design: just taken down from the shelf, dusted off, and re-applied to our new, digital medium.

Some of that recycling is perfectly natural. We're creatures of habit, after all: as soon as we move into a new city, or start a new job, we're mapping previous experiences onto the new, more

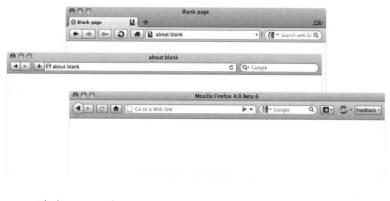

FIG 1.2: The browser window, our true canvas. (For better or worse.)

foreign one, using them to gradually orient ourselves. And since the web *is* a young medium, it's only natural to borrow some terms from what we know: graphic design provides us with a rich history that spans centuries, and we'd be remiss not to use its language to help shape our industry.

But our debt to print goes much deeper than language. In fact, there's another concept we've borrowed, one we might not acknowledge all that often: the canvas (FIG 1.1).

In every other creative medium, the artist begins her work by selecting a canvas. A painter chooses a sheet of paper or fabric to work on; a sculptor might select a block of stone from a quarry. Regardless of the medium, choosing a canvas is a powerful, creative act: before the first brush stroke, before striking the chisel, the canvas gives the art a dimension and shape, a width and a height, establishing a boundary for the work yet to come.

On the web, we try to mimic this process. We even call it the same thing: we create a "canvas" in our favorite image editor, a blank document with a width and height, with dimension and shape. The problem with this approach is that we're one step removed from our *actual* canvas: the browser window, and all of its inconsistencies and imperfections (FIG 1.2). Because let's face it: once they're published online, our designs are immediately at the mercy of the people who view them—to their font

FIG 1.3: Deviating slightly from our "ideal" parameters can negatively impact the user...

settings, to the color of their displays, to the shape and size of their browser windows.

So in the face of all that uncertainty, that flexibility, we begin by establishing constraints: we set our type in pixels, or create fixed-width layouts that assume a minimum screen resolution. Establishing those constraints is a bit like selecting a canvas—they give us known parameters to work from, certainties that help quarantine our work from the web's inherent flexibility.

But the best thing—and often, the worst thing—about the web is that it defies easy definition. If I were feeling especially bitter, I'd even go so far as to say it revels in its ability to shrug off whatever constraints we place around it. And the parameters we place on our designs are no different: they're easily broken. If a browser drops even slightly below our expected minimum width (**FIG 1.3**), a site's visitor might find her reading experience

FIG 1.4: ...or our businesses and clients. (What's a "reg," you ask? That's the "Register Now" link, hidden from view.)

is altered by a horizontal scrollbar and clipped content. But our businesses and clients could be affected as well (**FIG 1.4**): by relying on a minimum screen resolution, the placement of critical links or elements can be incredibly fragile, clipped by a viewport that obeys the user's preferences, not ours.

FASTEN THOSE SEATBELTS

More than a decade ago, John Allsopp wrote "A Dao of Web Design" (http://bkaprt.com/rwd2/3/), an article that, if you haven't read it, you should absolutely check out now. (Seriously. I'll wait.) It's easily my favorite essay about designing for the web, and it's just as relevant today as it was when it was first written. John argues that

> [t]he control which designers know in the print medium, and often desire in the web medium, is simply a function of the limitation of the printed page. We should embrace the fact that the web doesn't have the same constraints, and design for this flexibility. But first, we must "accept the ebb and flow of things."

Now, John was writing during the web's early years, a period of transition when designers transferred print-centered design principles onto this young, new medium. But much of what he wrote in the spring of 2000 still rings true today. Because the web has never felt more in flux, more variable than it does right now. After all, we've been entering our own transition period for some time. We're now faced with a browser landscape that's become almost entirely untethered from the desktop, with devices becoming smaller *and* larger simultaneously. Small-screen devices are quickly becoming the dominant form of web access (http://bkaprt.com/rwd2/4/), while modern game consoles have made a widescreen, television-centric web more readily accessible (http://bkaprt.com/rwd2/5/). Smart televisions allow owners to browse the web from the comfort of their couch, while web-connected, wearable gadgets are garnering significant interest. And tablet computing has become wildly popular in the past few years, presenting us with a mode of web access that is neither fully "mobile" nor "desktop," but somewhere in between.

The long and short of it is that we're designing for more devices, more input types, more *resolutions* than ever before. The web has moved beyond the desktop, and it's not turning back.

Unfortunately, our early attempts at designing beyond the desktop have felt pretty similar to our old approaches, applying constraints in the face of uncertainty. A few months ago, a friend emailed me a link to an article she'd just read on her phone:

http://mobile.seattletimes.com/story/today/2023429038/

See the word mobile in the link? The site's owners had quarantined the "mobile experience" on a separate URL, assuming it would only ever be viewed on a narrow, handheld screen. But whenever that link is shared on Twitter, Facebook, or via email, visitors will be locked into that small-screen-friendly view, regardless of the device they use to read it. And speaking for myself, the reading experience was, well, awful on a desktop browser.

That's not to say that mobile websites are inherently flawed, or that there aren't valid business cases for creating them. But I do think fragmenting our content across different "device-optimized" experiences is a losing proposition, or at least an unsustainable one. As the past few years have shown us, we simply can't compete with the pace of technology. Are we really going to create a custom experience for every new browser or device that appears? And if not, what's the alternative?

RESPONSIVE ARCHITECTURE

I've been an amateur fan of architecture for as long as I can remember. And as a web designer, there's something appealing about the number of constraints that architects seem to enjoy: from sketch to schematic, from foundation to façade, every step of the architectural process is more permanent than the one that preceded it. In *Parentalia,* the English architect Christopher Wren wrote that "architecture aims at eternity," and there's something to that: an architect's creative decisions will stand for decades, perhaps centuries.

After a day spent cursing at Internet Explorer, that kind of constancy sounds really, *really* nice.

But in recent years, a relatively new design discipline called "responsive architecture" has been challenging some of the permanence at the heart of the architectural discipline. It's a very young discipline, but this more interactive form has already manifested itself in several interesting ways.

Artists have experimented with surfaces that react to your voice with a music of their own (http://bkaprt.com/rwd2/6/), and with living spaces that can reform themselves to better fit their occupants (http://bkaprt.com/rwd2/7/). One company has produced "smart glass technology" that can become opaque once a room's occupants reach a certain density threshold, affording them an additional layer of privacy (**FIG 1.5**). And by combining tensile materials and embedded robotics, a German design consultancy has created a "wall" that can bend and flex as people approach it, potentially creating more or less space as the size of the crowd requires (**FIG 1.6**).

Rather than creating spaces that influence the behavior of people that pass through them, responsive designers are investigating ways for a piece of architecture and its inhabitants to mutually influence and inform each other.

FIG 1.5: Now you see it, now you don't: smart glass can be configured to become opaque automatically (http://bkaprt.com/rwd2/8/).

THE WAY FORWARD

What's fascinating to me is that architects are trying to overcome the constraints inherent to their medium. But web designers, facing a changing landscape of new devices and contexts, are now forced to overcome the constraints we've imposed on the web's innate flexibility.

We need to let go.

Rather than creating disconnected designs, each tailored to a particular device or browser, we should instead treat them as facets of the same experience. In other words, we can craft sites that are not only more flexible, but that can adapt to the media that renders them.

In short, we need to practice **responsive web design.** We can embrace the flexibility inherent to the web, without surrendering the control we require as designers. All by embedding standards-based technologies in our work, and by making a slight change in our philosophy toward online design.

FIG 1.6: It doesn't just make for an attractive art installation. This wall can actually detect your presence, and reshape itself to respond to your proximity (http://bkaprt.com/rwd2/9/).

The ingredients

So what does it take to create a responsive design? Speaking purely in terms of front-end layout, it takes three core ingredients:

1. **A flexible, grid-based layout,**
2. **Flexible images and media,** and
3. **Media queries,** a module from the CSS3 specification.

In the next three chapters, we'll look at each in turn—the flexible grid, fluid images and media, and CSS3 media queries—creating a more flexible, more responsive approach to designing for the web. As we do so, we'll have created a design that can adapt to the constraints of the browser window or device that renders it, creating a design that almost *responds* to the user's needs.

And here's the thing: as you work on your first responsive design, you're going to be in great company. Sites from nearly every industry have begun designing responsively, and stunningly

FIG 1.7: Many designers—including folks like Frank Chimero (http://frankchimero.com/), Trent Walton (http://trentwalton.com/), and Meagan Fisher (http://owltastic.com/)—are using responsive design to showcase their work, and tell stories that look beautiful on any screen.

so: from personal sites (FIG 1.7) to major, content-rich publications (FIG 1.8), from e-commerce storefronts (FIG 1.9) to media-heavy sites (FIG 1.10). Each is using flexible grids, flexible media, and media queries to create sites that aren't optimized solely for "mobile," "tablet," or "desktop," but are accessible—and beautiful!—regardless of the size of your screen.

In other words, it's a *great* time to be a responsive web designer.

So: let's dive in! But before we do, I should probably come clean: I'm a bit of a science fiction nut. I love me some laser pistols, androids, and flying cars, as well as movies and television shows containing copious amounts thereof. And I don't much care about the quality of said shows and movies, honestly. Whether directed by Kubrick or sporting a budget lower than

FIG 1.8: Publishers like Time.com and *The Boston Globe* have launched full responsive redesigns, while the responsive sites for BBC News and *The Guardian* are in public beta.

what I paid for lunch, I'll watch it: just make sure there's at least one rocket ship, and I'm happy.

In all the sci-fi I've watched, good or bad, there's a narrative device that genre writers really seem to love: the secret robot. I'm sure you've come across yarns like this before. They always start with a plucky band of adventurers trying to overcome some faceless evil, lead by some upstanding hero type, armed with pithy one-liners and/or steely resolve. But lurking somewhere within their ranks is...*a secret robot.* (Cue ominous music.) This devious, devilish device is an unfeeling being, wrought from cold steel and colder calculations, but made to look like a human, and it has a decidedly nefarious purpose: to take our band of heroes down from the inside.

FIG 1.9: From Coop (http://coop.se/) to Walmart.ca, from Skinny Ties (http://skinnyties .com/) to Expedia's responsive homepage (http://expedia.com/), e-commerce sites both large and small are designing responsively.

The revelation of the secret robot is where the story gets most of its drama. You know the hero, and you know the robotic spy, sure. But among the rest of the characters, you're always left asking yourself: who is, and who isn't, a robot?

Personally, I've never understood why this is so hard. Me, I miss the days of Johnny 5 and C-3PO, when you knew a robot by just looking at it, with none of this "skulking around in synthetic skin" nonsense. So I've taken matters into my own hands: to clear up some of this confusion, I've designed a simple little site called "Robot or Not" (**FIG 1.11**). It's intended to help us identify who exactly is, and is not, a robot. To help us better tell fleshy friend from ferrous foe.

Okay, maybe I'm the only one who has this problem.

FIG 1.8: Disney's corporate site (http://disney.com/) features an impressive amount of video in a responsive design, while the site promoting electronic duo George & Jonathan (http://www.georgeandjonathan.com/) is an immersive—and responsive!—experience.

But regardless of how useful this site will actually be, we'll use its modest little design to demonstrate exactly how a responsive site is built. Over the next few chapters, we'll be developing Robot or Not together, using flexible grids, flexible images, and media queries.

Now, maybe you're not one for suspense. Or, more likely, maybe you're already tired of hearing me blather on at length, and just want to see the finished product. If that's the case, then simply point your browser to http://responsivewebdesign.com/robot/, and feel free to kick the tires a bit. What's more, the code is available for download at http://bkaprt.com/rwd2/10/, if you'd like to play along at home.

Still here? Great. Let's get started.

FIG 1.11: The design for Robot or Not, in all its beeping, bitmappy glory.

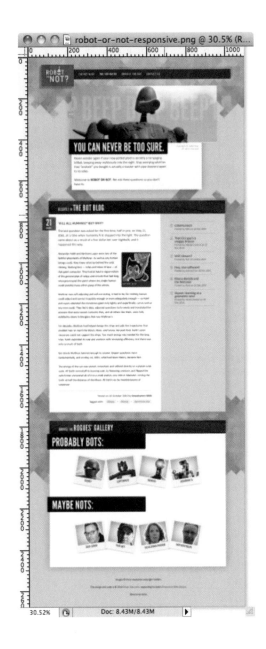

THE FLEXIBLE GRID

WHEN I WAS in college, a professor once told me that every artistic movement—whether musical, literary, or from the fine arts—could be seen as a response to the one that preceded it. Filmmakers of the sixties produced *Bonnie and Clyde* and *The Graduate* to counter such old Hollywood pictures as *The Sound of Music*. In *Paradise Lost,* John Milton actually writes his literary predecessors into the backdrop of hell—a not-so-subtle dig at their poetic street cred. And if it weren't for the tight arrangements of Duke Ellington and Benny Goodman, Charlie Parker might never have produced the wild-eyed experimentation of bebop.

One artist establishes a point; another sets the counterpoint. And this was especially true for the artists of the Modernist period in the mid-20th century. The Modernists were looking at the creative output of *their* predecessors, the Romantic period of the late 19th century, with, well, a little disdain. To them, Romantic

FIG 2.1: The Modernists heralded a shift away from the embellished realism of William Blake and Eugène Delacroix, to the more rational approach of Hans Hofmann and Josef Müller-Brockmann.

art was just laden down with all this *stuff*—needless, embellished ornamentation that overwhelmed the artwork, and impeded its ability to properly communicate with the viewer (**FIG 2.1**).

Now, the Modernist reaction to this took many different forms, spanning nearly every artistic medium. In painting, this meant reducing works to experiments in line, shape, and color. But graphic designers of the period, like Jan Tschichold, Emil Ruder, and Josef Müller-Brockmann, popularized this concept of a typographic grid: a rational system of columns and rows, upon which modules of content could be placed (**FIG 2.2**). And thanks to designers like Khoi Vinh and Mark Boulton, we've managed to adapt this old concept to the needs of contemporary web design.

In his book *Grid Systems in Graphic Design,* Müller-Brockmann referred to this process as "creating a typographic space on the page," tailoring the proportions of the grid to the size of a blank piece of paper. But for a web designer, we're missing one key component: the presence of an actual page. Our canvas, the browser window, can bend and flex to any shape or size, whether changed at the whim of the reader, or fixed by the phone or tablet they're using to view our content.

Often, the first layer of our grid-based layouts looks like this:

Vermont Symphony Orchestra

Winter 2007 Season	Aaron Copland **The Tender Land** January 2007	Eric Satie **Gymnopedie 1, 2** February 2007
	01/12/07 **Middlebury College Center for the Arts** 8:00 pm	02/03/07 **Johnson State College Dibden Center for the Arts** 8:00 pm
	01/19/07 **Johnson State College Dibden Center for the Arts** 8:00 pm	02/10/07 **Castleton State College Fine Arts Center** 8:00 pm
	01/26/07 **Lyndon State College Alexander Twilight Theater** 8:00 pm	02/17/07 **Middlebury College Center for the Arts** 8:00 pm

FIG 2.2: When tailored to the needs of your content as well as the page's dimensions, the typographic grid is a powerful tool, aiding designer and reader alike.

```
.page {
  width: 960px;
  margin: 0 auto;
}
```

We create an element in our markup, give it a fixed width in our CSS, and center it in the page. But when we're thinking flexibly, we instead need to translate a design created in Photoshop (**FIG 2.3**) into something more fluid, something more *proportional.* How do we begin?

FLEXIBLE TYPESETTING

To find an answer, let's do a little role-playing. No, no—you can put away those twenty-sided dice. I had something a bit more practical (and a bit less orc-enabled) in mind.

Pretend for a moment that you're working as a front-end developer. (If you're already a front-end developer, well, pretend

FIG 2.3: Our PSD is looking pretty, but that grid's more than slightly pixel-heavy. How can we become more flexible?

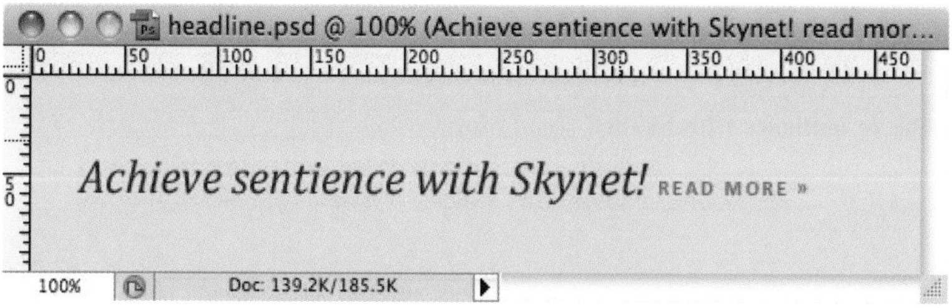

FIG 2.4: The mockup for our typesetting exercise. This should take, like, minutes.

you're also wearing a pirate hat.) A designer on your team has asked you to convert a simple design into markup and CSS. Always game to help out, you take a quick look at the PSD she sent you (**FIG 2.4**).

There's not much content here, true. But hey—even short jobs require close attention to detail, so you begin focusing on the task at hand. And after carefully assessing the content types in the mockup, here's the HTML you come up with:

```
<h1>Achieve sentience with Skynet! <a href="#">Read  »
    More &raquo;</a></h1>
```

A headline with a link embedded in it—a fine foundation of semantic markup, don't you think? After dropping in a reset stylesheet, the content begins shaping up in your browser (**FIG 2.5**).

It's definitely a modest start. But with our foundation in place, we can begin adding a layer of style. Let's start by applying some basic rules to the body element:

```
body {
    background-color: #DCDBD9;
    color: #2C2C2C;
    font: normal 100% Cambria, Georgia, serif;
}
```

Nothing too fancy: We're applying a light gray background color (#DCDBD9) to our entire document, and a fairly dark text

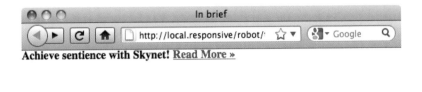

In brief

http://local.responsive/robot/   Google

Achieve sentience with Skynet! Read More »

Done

FIG 2.5: Plain, style-free markup. The stuff dreams (and websites) are made of.

color (#2C2C2C). And finally, we've dropped in the font characteristics: a default weight (normal), and a serif-heavy font stack
(Cambria, Georgia, serif).

Finally, you've probably noticed that the font-size has been
set to 100%. In doing so, we've simply set our base type size to
the browser's default, which in most cases is 16 pixels. We can
then use ems to size text up or down from that relative baseline.
But before we do, we can see that our headline's starting to shape
up (**FIG 2.6**).

Wondering why the h1 doesn't look, well, headline-y? We're
currently using a reset stylesheet, which overrides a browser's
default styles for HTML elements. It's a handy way to get all
browsers working from a consistent baseline. Personally, I'm
a big fan of Eric Meyer's reset (http://bkaprt.com/rwd2/11/), but
there are dozens of fine alternatives out there.

At any rate, that's why our h1 looks so small: it's simply inheriting the font-size of 100% we set on the body element, and
rendering at the browser's default type size of 16 pixels.

Now, if we were content with pixels, we could just translate
the values from the comp directly into our CSS:

```
h1 {
  font-size: 24px;
  font-style: italic;
  font-weight: normal;
}
```

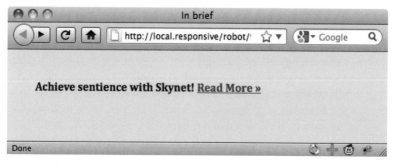

FIG 2.6: With one simple CSS rule, we can set some high-level parameters for our design.

```
h1 a {
    color: #747474;
    font: bold 11px Calibri, Optima, Arial, sans-serif;
    letter-spacing: 0.15em;
    text-transform: uppercase;
    text-decoration: none;
}
```

And that would be fine—there's nothing actually *wrong* with setting your type in pixels. But for the purposes of our relative typesetting experiment, let's instead start to think proportionally, and express those pixel-based font-size values in relative terms. So instead of pixels, we'll use our friend the em.

Contextual healing

To do so, we'll need to do a teensy bit of math: we'll simply take the *target* font size from our comp, and divide it by the font-size of its containing element—in other words, its *context*. The *result* is our desired font-size expressed in relative, oh-so-flexible ems.

In other words, relative type sizes can be calculated with this simple formula:

```
target ÷ context = result
```

(Quick aside: If you're at all like me, the word "math" causes immediate and serious panic. But speaking as someone who took a philosophy course for his college math credit, don't run screaming into the hills quite yet. I rely on my computer's calculator program heavily, and simply paste the result into my CSS. That keeps me from really having to, you know, *do* the math.)

So with our formula in hand, let's turn back to that 24px headline. Assuming that our base font-size: 100% on the body element equates to 16px, we can plug those values directly into our formula. So if we need to express our h1's target font size (24px) relative to its context (16px), we get:

```
24 ÷ 16 = 1.5
```

And there we are: 24px is 1.5 times greater than 16px, so our font-size is 1.5em:

```
h1 {
    font-size: 1.5em;   /* 24px / 16px */
    font-style: italic;
    font-weight: normal;
}
```

And *voilà!* Our headline's size perfectly matches the size specified in our comp, but is expressed in relative, scaleable terms (**FIG 2.7**).

(I usually put the math behind my measurements in a comment to the right-hand side of the line (/* 24px / 16px */), which makes future adjustments much, much easier for me to make.)

With that squared away, let's turn to our lonely little "Read More" link. Actually, as you can see in **FIGURE 2.7**, it's *not* so little—and that's the problem. Sized in our comp (**FIG 2.4**) at 11 pixels in a generously kerned sans-serif, we need to scale the text down. A lot. Because at the moment, it's simply inheriting the font-size: 1.5em set on its containing element, the h1.

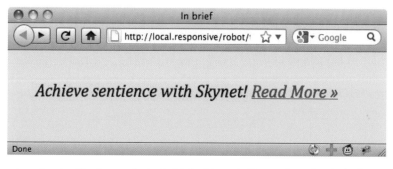

And that's important to note. Because the headline's text is set at 1.5em, any elements inside that headline need to be expressed in relation to that value. In other words, *our context has changed.*

So to set the font-size of our link in ems, we'll divide our target of 11px not by 16px, the value set on the body, but by 24px—the font size of the headline, our new context:

```
11 ÷ 24 = 0.458333333333333
```

After that little division we're left with one of the least sexy numbers you've probably seen yet today. (Oh, but just you wait: the chapter's not over yet.)

Now, you might be tempted to round 0.45833333333333em to the nearest sane-looking number—say, to 0.46em. But don't touch that delete key! It might make your eyes bleed to look at it, but 0.458333333333333 perfectly represents our desired font size in proportional terms. What's more, browsers are perfectly adept at rounding off those excess decimal places as they internally convert the values to pixels. So giving them more information, not less, will net you a better result in the end.

In the spirit of accuracy, we can just drop that homely-looking number directly into our CSS *(line wraps marked »):*

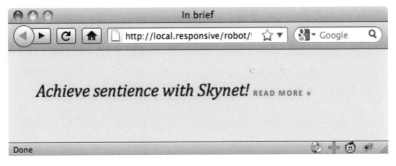

FIG 2.8: And with some simple math, our typesetting's complete—without a single pixel in sight.

```
h1 a {
  font: bold 0.458333333333333em Calibri, Optima,  »
    Arial, sans-serif;  /* 11px / 24px */
  color: #747474;
  letter-spacing: 0.15em;
  text-transform: uppercase;
  text-decoration: none;
}
```

The result? Our tiny page is finished, perfectly matching our intended design—but with text set in resizable, scalable ems (**FIG 2.8**).

From flexible fonts to a flexible grid

It's possible you're very, very bored right now. I mean, here you are, knee-deep in what's *supposed* to be a chapter about creating flexible, grid-based layouts, and this Ethan fellow won't stop prattling on about *typesetting* and *math*. The nerve.

But the first time I had to build on a flexible grid, I had no idea where to begin. So I did what I do every time I'm faced with a problem I don't know how to solve: I avoided it entirely, and started working on something else.

As I started work on setting the site's type in ems, I had a minor epiphany: namely, that we can apply the same sort of proportional thinking to layout that we apply to relative font sizes. In other words, every aspect of our grid—the rows and columns, and the modules draped over them—can be expressed as *proportions* of their containing element, rather than in unchanging, inflexible pixels.

And we can do so by recycling our trusty `target ÷ context = result` formula. Let's dive in.

CREATING A FLEXIBLE GRID

Let's pretend that our designer sent over another mockup, since she was so impressed with our quick turnaround on that headline we produced. We're now tasked with coding the blog section of the Robot or Not website (**FIG 2.9**).

As it turns out, our designer likes us so darn much she's even included a quick content inventory of the page (**FIG 2.10**), which will save us some pre-production planning. We should really send her some cookies or something.

We can handily translate her schematic into a basic markup structure, like so:

```
<div class="page">
  <div class="blog section">
    <h1 class="lede">Recently in <a href="#">The Bot  »
    Blog</a></h1>

    <div class="main">
      …
    </div><!-- /end .main -->

    <div class="other">
      …
    </div><!-- /end .other -->
  </div><!-- /end .blog.section -->
</div><!-- /end .page -->
```

FIG 2.9: Our new assignment: converting this blog design into a standards-based, *flexible* layout.

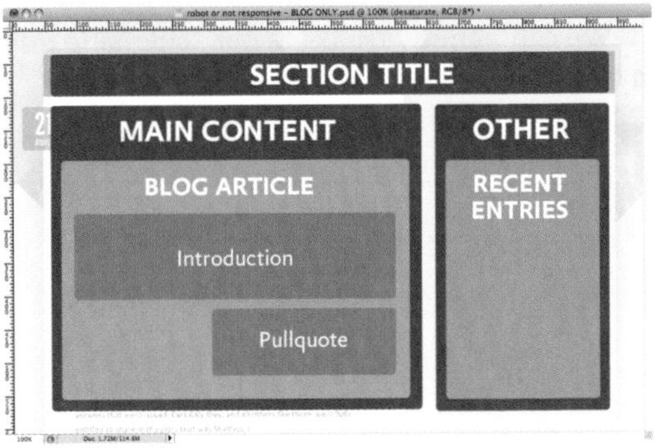

FIG 2.10: The content inventory for our blog module.

Our skeleton markup is lean, mean, and semantically rich, perfectly matching the high-level content inventory. We've created a generic container for the entire page (`.page`), which in turn contains our `.blog` module. And within `.blog` we've created two more containers: a `div` classed as `.main` for our main article content, and another `div` classed as `.other` for, um, other stuff. Poetry it ain't, but poetry it doesn't have to be.

At this point, we're going to skip a few steps in our exercise. In fact, let's pretend that this is one of those cooking shows where the chef throws a bunch of ingredients into a pot, and then turns around to produce a fully cooked turkey. (This metaphor handily demonstrates how infrequently I watch cooking shows. Or cook turkey.)

But let's assume that we've already done all the CSS related to typesetting, background images, and just about every element of our design that *isn't* related to layout (**FIG 2.11**). With those other details finished, we can focus exclusively on producing our fluid grid.

So how exactly do we turn those .main and .other blocks into proper columns? With our content inventory finished and some basic markup in place, let's go back to our comp and take a closer look at the grid's physical characteristics (**FIG 2.12**).

Reviewing the design tells us a few things: first, that the grid itself is divided into 12 columns, each measuring 69 pixels across and separated by regular `12px`-wide gutters. Taken together, those columns and gutters give us a total width of 960 pixels. However, the blog itself is only 900 pixels wide, centered horizontally within that `960px`-wide canvas.

So those are the high-level details. And if we take a closer look at the two columns inside of the blog (**FIG 2.13**), we can see that the left-hand content column (`.main` in our markup) is 566 pixels wide, while the right-hand, secondary column (`.other`) is only 331 pixels across.

Well now. Quite a few pixel values floating around so far, aren't there? And if we were content with pixels we could simply drop them into our CSS directly. (Hel*lo*, leading statement!)

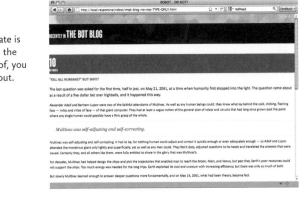

FIG 2.11: Our template is finished! Well, with the possible exception of, you know, an actual layout.

```
.page {
  margin: 36px auto;
  width: 960px;
}

.blog {
  margin: 0 auto 53px;
  width: 900px;
}

.blog .main {
  float: left;
  width: 566px;
}

.blog .other {
  float: right;
  width: 331px;
}
```

Nice and neat: we've set the width of .page to 960 pixels, centered the 900px-wide .blog module within that container, set the widths of .main and .other to 566px and 331px, respectively,

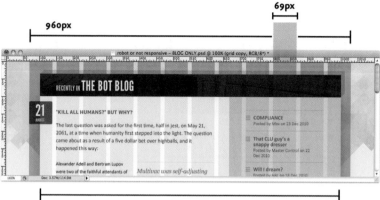

FIG 2.12: Grid-based layout is grid-based!

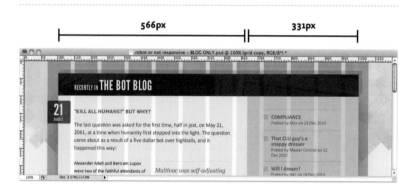

FIG 2.13: Let's narrow our focus a bit, and measure the internal columns.

and finally floated the two columns opposite each other. And the result looks stellar (FIG 2.14).

But while our layout's matched the comp perfectly, the result is downright inflexible. Fixed at a width of 960px, our page is blissfully indifferent to changes in viewport size, forcing a horizontal scrollbar upon the reader if the window drops even slightly below 1024 pixels (FIG 2.15).

In short, we can do better.

FIG 2.14: A few pixel-based floats later, and our design's nearly finished. Or is it?

From pixels to percentages

Instead of pasting the pixel values from our comp directly into our CSS, we need to express those widths in relative, *proportional* terms. Once we've done so, we'll have a grid that can resize itself as the viewport does, but without compromising the design's original proportions.

Let's start at the outermost .page element, which contains our design, and work our way in:

```
.page {
  margin: 36px auto;
  width: 960px;
}
```

Nasty, evil pixels. We hates them.

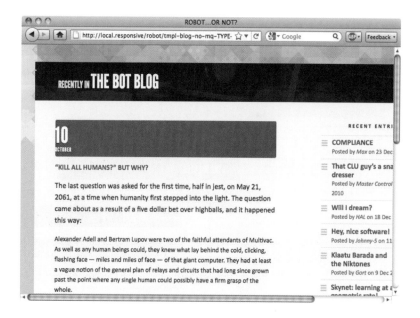

FIG 2.15: Our layout is lovely, but it's so very inflexible. Let's fix that.

Okay, okay: not really. Remember, there's absolutely nothing wrong with fixed-width layouts! But to move toward a more flexible grid, let's start with a percentage value to replace that 960px:

```
.page {
    margin: 36px auto;
    width: 90%;
}
```

I'll confess that I arrived at 90% somewhat arbitrarily, doing a bit of trial and error in the browser window to see what looked best. By setting our .page element to a percentage of the browser window, we've created a container that will expand and contract as the viewport does (FIG 2.16). And as that container is centered horizontally within the page, we'll be left with a comfortable five percent margin on either side.

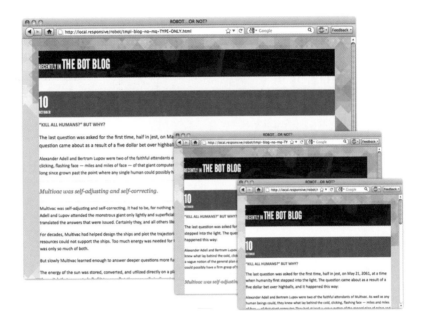

FIG 2.16: Our container flexes as the browser window does.

So far, so good. Moving down the markup, let's set our sights on the `.blog` module itself. Previously, when we were toying with pixels, we wrote the following rule:

```
.blog {
  margin: 0 auto 53px;
  width: 900px;
}
```

Instead of a value set in pixels, we need to express `.blog`'s width of `900px` in proportional terms: specifically, describing it as a percentage of the width of its containing element. And this is where our beloved `target ÷ context = result` formula comes back into play.

We already know our *target* pixel width for our blog: that's `900px`, as defined in our mockup. What we want is to describe that width in relative terms, as a percentage of .blog's containing element. Since .blog is nested within the .page element, we've got our *context*—namely, 960 pixels, the width of .page as it was designed in the mockup.

So let's divide our target width for .blog (900) by its context (960):

```
900 ÷ 960 = 0.9375
```

We're left with a result of 0.9375. Doesn't look like much, I'll admit. But by moving the decimal over two places we're left with 93.75%, a percentage we can drop directly into our CSS:

```
.blog {
  margin: 0 auto 53px;
  width: 93.75%;   /* 900px / 960px */
}
```

(Just as I did with our relative typesetting exercise, I've left the formula in a comment off to the right of the width property. This is a personal preference, of course, but I've found it to be incredibly helpful.)

So that takes care of our two containing elements. But what about our content columns?

```
.blog .main {
  float: left;
  width: 566px;
}

.blog .other {
  float: right;
  width: 331px;
}
```

Our left-hand content column is floated to the left, and set at 566px; the additional content is floated opposite, sized at a width of 331px. Once again, let's replace those pixel-based target widths with percentages.

But before we drop those values into our target ÷ context = result formula, it's important to note that *our context has changed.* Last time, we divided the width of our blog module by 960px, the width of its container (.page). But since they're nested inside .blog, we need to express our columns' widths in relation to 900px—the width of the blog.

So we'll divide our two target values (566px and 331px) by 900px, our new context:

```
566 ÷ 900 = .628888889
331 ÷ 900 = .367777778
```

Once we move our decimal points we're left with 62.8888889% and 36.7777778%, the proportional widths of .main and .other:

```
.blog .main {
  float: left;
  width: 62.8888889%;   /* 566px / 900px */
}

.blog .other {
  float: right;
  width: 36.7777778%;   /* 331px / 900px */
}
```

Just like that, we're left with a flexible, grid-based layout (**FIG 2.17**).

With some simple math we've created a percentage-based container and two flexible columns, creating a layout that resizes in concert with the browser window. And as it does, the pixel widths of those columns might change—but the *proportions* of our design remain intact.

FLEXIBLE MARGINS AND PADDING

Now that those two columns are in place, we're done with the top-level components of our flexible grid. Marvelous. Wonderful. Stupendous, even. But before we haul out any more adjectives, there's quite a bit of detail work to be done.

FIG 2.17: Our flexible grid is complete.

Can't get no ventilation

First and foremost, our design may be flexible, but it is in *serious* need of some detail work. The two most grievous offenders? The title of our blog is flush left within its container (**FIG 2.18**), and our two columns currently abut each other, with no margins or gutters in sight (**FIG 2.19**). We definitely have some cleanup to do.

So let's begin with that headline. In our comp, there's 48 pixels of space between our headline and the left edge of its container (**FIG 2.20**). Now, we *could* use pixels to set a fixed `padding-left` on our headline in either pixels or ems, like so:

```
.lede {
    padding: 0.8em 48px;
}
```

This is a decent solution. But a fixed value for that `padding-left` would create a gutter that doesn't line up with the rest of our fluid grid. As our flexible columns expand or contract, that gutter would simply ignore the rest of our design's proportions, sitting stubbornly at `48px` no matter how small or wide the design became.

So instead, let's create a flexible gutter. So far, we've been describing various elements' widths in proportional terms. But we can also create percentage-based margins and padding to preserve the integrity of our flexible grid. And we can reuse the `target ÷ context = result` formula to do so.

Before we start in with the math, it's important to note that whether you're setting a flexible margin or padding on an

FIG 2.18: Our headline is in dire need of padding.

FIG 2.19: Margins? We don't need no stinking margins. (Actually, we do. We really do.)

Aultivac. As well as

ning face — miles

n of the general

ny single human

≡ **Hey, n**
Posted I

≡ **Klaatu**
Posted I

≡ **Skyne**
Posted I

FIG 2.20: According to the design, we need 48px of horizontal padding on the left edge of our headline.

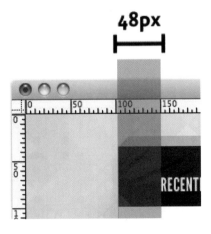

element, the context is always the same: it's the width of the element's container.

Since we want to set some padding on our .lede headline, our context is the width of its container—that is, our 900px-wide .blog module. So out comes the calculator, and we're left with:

```
48 ÷ 900 = 0.0533333333
```

which translates to:

```
.lede {
    padding: 0.8em 5.33333333%;  /* 48px / 900px */
}
```

And there we have it: our 48px padding has been expressed in relative terms, as a proportion of our headline's width.

With that issue resolved, let's introduce a bit of white space to our compacted content. To do so, it's worth remembering that each column actually has a smaller module contained within it: the left-hand .blog column contains an .article, while the .other column contains our .recent-entries listing (**FIG 2.21**). We start with the recent entries module. Fortunately for us, our work's over pretty quickly. Since we know the width of the element (231px) and the width of its containing column (331px), we can simply center our module horizontally:

```
.recent-entries {
    margin: 0 auto;
    width: 69.7885196%;  /* 231px / 331px */
}
```

Now, we could take the same approach with our article. But instead, let's make it a bit more interesting. Remember the 48px padding we set on our headline? Well, our article falls along the same column (**FIG 2.22**). So rather than just centering our article within its container, let's create another proportional gutter.

Our target value is 48px. And since we're working with relative padding, our context should be the width of the article itself.

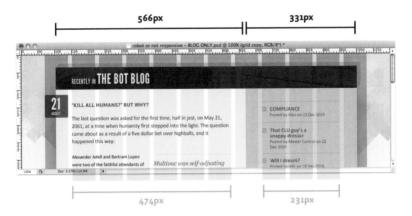

FIG 2.21: Taking a look at the comp, we can quickly size up their respective widths. Pun unfortunate, but intended.

FIG 2.22: Our headline and article share a common padding.

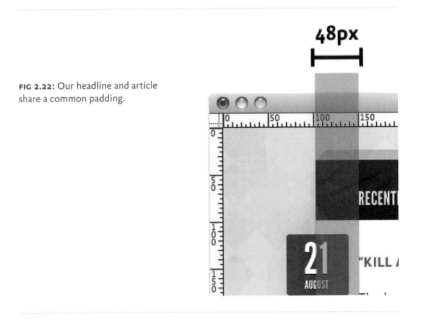

But once again, since there's no explicit width set on `.article`, we can simply use 566px, the width of its parent (`.blog`), for our context:

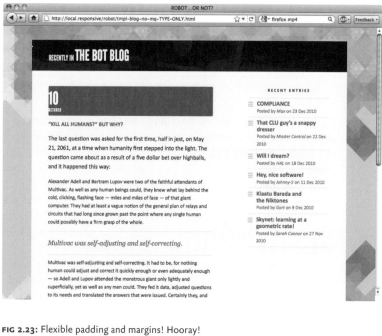

FIG 2.23: Flexible padding and margins! Hooray!

```
.article {
  padding: 40px 8.48056537%;  /* 48px / 566px */
}
```

Voilà! Our flexible grid's all but finished (**FIG 2.23**).

Getting negative

Let's turn to our blog entry's beleaguered date header. Currently, it's spanning the full width of the blog entry, and that won't do. Given what we've learned so far, it's fairly straightforward to fix its width: the comp tells us our date should be floated to the left, and that it occupies one 69px column (refer back to **FIG 2.21**). Since the date sits within the 470px-wide article, we have our context.

Armed with that information, let's write some quick CSS:

```
.date {
  float: left;
  width: 14.68085106%;   /* 69px / 470px */
}
```

So far, so flexible, so good. But there's one key component miss-ing: our date is currently floating neatly against the left edge of the article, with the title and copy floating around it (**FIG 2.24**). What we need to do is to pull that date out of its container, and move it across the left-hand edge of the entire module.

And with negative margins, we can do exactly that. And we don't have to change our approach because the margin is nega-tive: just as before, we simply need to express that margin in relation to the width of the element's container.

If we look at the mockup, we can see that there are 81 pixels from the left edge of the date over to the left edge of the article (**FIG 2.25**). And if this was a fixed-width design, that would be our negative margin:

```
.date {
  float: left;
  margin-left: -81px;
  width: 69px;
}
```

But hey: we haven't used a single pixel yet, and we're not about to start now. Instead, we want to express that margin in relative terms. It's going to be a negative margin, but that doesn't change the math. We still want to express our target value—that 81px-wide margin—as a percentage of 470px, the width of the date's containing element:

```
81 ÷ 470 = .17234042553191
```

Do the decimal shift and slap a minus sign on there, and we've got our proportional, negative margin:

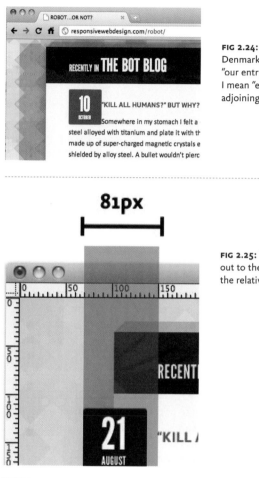

FIG 2.24: Something's rotten in Denmark. (By "Denmark," I mean "our entry date." And by "rotten," I mean "entirely too close to the adjoining text.")

FIG 2.25: We need to draw that date out to the left by 81px. Or, you know, the relative equivalent thereof.

```
.date {
  float: left;
  margin-left: -17.2340425531%;   /* 81px / 470px */
  width: 14.68085106%;   /* 69px / 470px */
}
```

Now sit back, relax, and take comfort in the fact that you've built your first fully flexible grid (**FIG 2.26**). I feel a high five coming on.

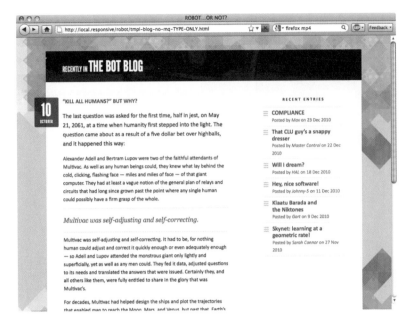

FIG 2.26: Our flexible grid is finally finished. Not a pixel value in sight, and we didn't have to skimp on the aesthetics.

Moving forward, flexibly

I realize I just subjected you to a truckload of division signs. And as someone who gets headaches from balancing his checkbook, believe me: I sympathize.

But building a flexible grid isn't entirely about the math. The `target ÷ context = result` formula makes it easy to articulate those proportions into stylesheet-ready percentages, sure—but ultimately, we need to break our habit of translating pixels from Photoshop directly into our CSS, and focus our attention on the proportions behind our designs. It's about becoming *context-aware:* better understanding the ratio-based relationships between element and container.

But a fluid grid is just our foundation; it's the first—but most important—layer of a responsive design. Let's move onto the next step.

3 FLEXIBLE IMAGES

THINGS ARE looking good so far: we've got a grid-based layout, one that doesn't sacrifice complexity for flexibility. I have to admit that the first time I figured out how to build a fluid grid, I was feeling pretty proud of myself.

But then, as often happens with web design, despair set in. Currently, our page is awash in words, and little else. Actually, *nothing* else: our page is nothing *but* text. Why is this a problem? Well, text reflows effortlessly within a flexible container—and I don't know if you've noticed, but the Internet seems to have one or two of those "image" things lying around. None of which we've incorporated into our fluid grid.

So what happens when we introduce fixed-width images into our flexible design?

GOING BACK, BACK TO MARKUP, MARKUP

To find an answer, let's do another quick experiment: let's drop an image directly into our blog module, and see how our layout responds. The first thing we'll need to do is to clear some space for it in our markup.

Remember our little blockquote, comfortably tucked into our blog article? Well, we've got *way* too much text on this darned page, so let's replace it with an inset image:

```
<div class="figure">
  <p>
    <img src="robot.jpg" alt="" />
    <b class="figcaption">Lo, the robot walks</b>
  </p>
</div>
```

Nothing fancy: an img element, followed by a brief but descriptive caption wrapped in a b element. I'm actually appropriating the HTML5 figure/figcaption tags as class names in this snippet, which makes for a solidly semantic foundation.

(Sharp-eyed readers will note that I'm using a b element for a non-semantic hook. Now, some designers might use a span element instead. Me, I like the terseness of shorter tags like b or i for non-semantic markup.)

With that HTML finished, let's drop in some basic CSS:

```
.figure {
  float: right;
  margin-bottom: 0.5em;
  margin-left: 2.55319149%;   /* 12px / 470px */
  width: 49.14893617%;   /* 231px / 470px */
}
```

We're creating a nice inset effect for our figure. It'll be floated to the right, and will span roughly half the width of our article, or four columns of our flexible grid. Markup: check; style: check. Of course, all this HTML and CSS is for naught if there isn't an actual *image* available.

Now, because I love you (and robots) dearly, not just *any* image will do. And after scouring the web for whole minutes, I found a fantastically imposing robo-portrait (**FIG 3.1**). The beautiful thing about this image (aside from the robot, of course) is that

FIG 3.1: An appropriately botty robot pic, courtesy of Jeremy Noble (http://bkaprt.com/rwd2/12/).

FIG 3.2: Our huge image is huge. Our broken layout is broken.

it's huge. I've cropped it slightly, but I haven't scaled it down at all, leaving it at its native resolution of 655×655. This image is much larger than we know its flexible container will be, making it a perfect case to test how robust our flexible layout is.

So let's drop our oversized image onto the server, reload the page, and—oh. Well. That's pretty much the worst thing on the internet (**FIG 3.2**).

Actually, the result isn't that surprising. Our layout isn't broken *per se*—our flexible container is working just fine, and the proportions of our grid's columns remain intact. But because our image is much wider than its containing .figure, the excess content simply overflows its container, and is visible to the user. There simply aren't any constraints applied to our image that could make it aware of its flexible environment.

FLUID IMAGES

But what if we could introduce such a constraint? What if we could write a rule that prevents images from exceeding the width of their container?

Well, here's the good news: that's very easy to do.

```
img {
  max-width: 100%;
}
```

First discovered by designer Richard Rutter (http://bkaprt.com/rwd2/13/), this one rule immediately provides an incredibly handy constraint for every image in our document. Now, our img element will render at whatever size it wants, as long as it's narrower than its containing element. But if it happens to be wider than its container, then the max-width: 100% directive forces the image's width to match the width of its container. And as you can see, our image has snapped into place (**FIG 3.3**).

What's more, modern browsers have evolved to the point where they resize the images proportionally: as our flexible container resizes itself, shrinking or enlarging our image, the image's aspect ratio remains intact (**FIG 3.4**).

I hope you're not tired of all this good news because as it happens, the max-width: 100% rule can also apply to most fixed-width elements, like video and other rich media. In fact, we can beef up our selector to cover other media-ready elements, like so:

```
img,
embed,
object,
video {
  max-width: 100%;
}
```

FIG 3.3: Just by including `max-width: 100%`, we've prevented our image from escaping its flexible container. On a related note, I love `max-width: 100%`.

Whether it's a cute little Flash video (**FIG 3.5**), some other embedded media, or a humble `img`, browsers do a fair job of resizing the content to fit a flexible layout. All thanks to our lightweight `max-width` constraint.

So we've cracked the problem of flexible images and media—right? One CSS rule and we're done?

BECAUSE THIS JOB IS NEVER EASY

Time to let the healing begin: we need to work through the pain, the tears, the rending of garments, and talk about a few browser-specific issues around flexible images.

FIG 3.4: Regardless of how wide or small its flexible container becomes, the image resizes proportionally. Magic? Who can say.

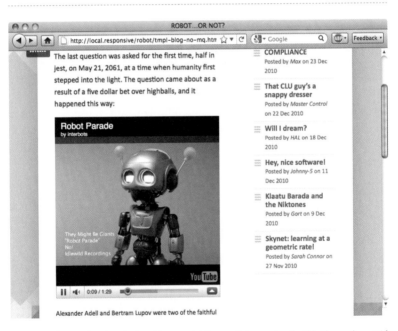

FIG 3.5: Other media play nicely with `max-width: 100%`, becoming flexible themselves. Did I mention I love `max-width: 100%`?

max-width in Internet Explorer

The cold, hard truth is that Internet Explorer 6 and below don't support the `max-width` property. IE7 version and above? Oh, it is positively brimming with support for `max-width`. But if you're stuck supporting the (cough) venerable IE6 or lower, our approach needs refinement.

Now, there are several documented ways to get max-width support working in IE6. Most are JavaScript-driven, usually relying on Microsoft's proprietary `expression` filter to dynamically evaluate the width of an element, and to manually resize it if it exceeds a certain threshold. For an example of these decidedly non-standard workarounds, I'd recommend Cameron Moll's classic blog entry on the subject (http://bkaprt.com/rwd2/14/).

Me? I tend to favor a more lo-fi, CSS-driven approach. Namely, all modern browsers get our max-width constraint:

```
img,
embed,
object,
video {
  max-width: 100%;
}
```

But in a separate IE6-specific stylesheet, I'll include the following:

```
img,
embed,
object,
video {
  width: 100%;
}
```

See the difference? IE6 and lower get `width: 100%`, rather than the `max-width: 100%` rule.

A word of warning: tread carefully here, for these are drastically different rules. Whereas `max-width: 100%` instructs our images to never exceed the width of their containers, `width:` `100%` forces our images to *always match* the width of their containing elements.

Most of the time, this approach will work just fine. For example, it's safe to assume that our oversized `robot.jpg` image will always be larger than its containing element, so the `width:` `100%` rule works beautifully.

But for smaller images like thumbnails, or most embedded movies, it might not be appropriate to blindly up-scale them with CSS. If that's the case, then a bit more specificity might be warranted for IE:

```
img.full,
object.full,
.main img,
.main object {
  width: 100%;
}
```

If you don't want the `width:` `100%` rule to apply to every piece of fixed-width media in your page, we can simply write a list of selectors that target certain kinds of images or video (`img.full`), or certain areas of your document where you know you'll be dealing with oversized media (`.main img, .main object`). Think of this like a whitelist: if images or other media appear on this list, then they'll be flexible; otherwise, they'll be fixed in their stodgy old pixel-y ways.

So if you're still supporting legacy versions of Internet Explorer, a carefully applied `width:` `100%` rule can get those flexible images working beautifully. But with that bug sorted, we've still got one to go.

And boy, it's a doozy.

In which it becomes clear that Windows hates us

If you look at our blog module with certain Windows-based browsers, our `robot.jpg` has gone from looking imposing to looking, well, broken (**FIG. 3.6**). But this isn't a browser-specific issue as much as a platform-specific one: Windows doesn't scale

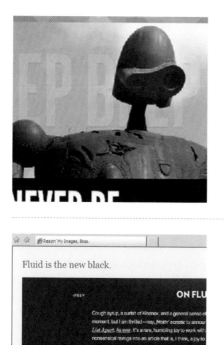

FIG 3.6: Seen here in IE6, our robot image has developed some unsightly artifacts. Guess Windows doesn't much care for our flexible images.

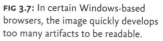

FIG 3.7: In certain Windows-based browsers, the image quickly develops too many artifacts to be readable.

images that well. In fact, when they're resized via CSS, images quickly develop artifacts on Windows, dramatically impacting their quality. And not in a good way.

For a quick test case, I've tossed a text-heavy graphic into a flexible container, and then resized our image with the `max-width: 100%` fix, while IE6 and below receive the `width: 100%` workaround. Now, you'd never actually put this amount of text in an image. But it perfectly illustrates just how badly things can get in IE7 or lower. As you can see, the image looks—if you'll pardon the technical term—downright nasty (**FIG 3.7**).

But before you give up on the promise of scalable, flexible images, it's worth noting that this bug doesn't affect every Windows-based browser. In fact, only Internet Explorer 7 and lower are affected, as is Firefox 2 and lower on Windows. More modern browsers like Safari, Firefox 3+, and IE8+ don't exhibit a single problem with flexible images. What's more, the bug seems to have been fixed in Windows 7, so that's more good news.

So with the scope of the problem defined, surely there's a patch we can apply? Thankfully, there is—with the exception of Firefox 2.

Now, this grizzled old browser was released in 2006, so I think it's safe to assume it isn't exactly clogging up your site's traffic logs. At any rate, a patch for Firefox 2 would require some fairly involved browser-sniffing to target specific versions on a specific platform—and browser-sniffing is unreliable at best. But even if we *did* want to perform that kind of detection, these older versions of Firefox don't have a switch that could fix our busted-looking images.

Internet Explorer, however, *does* have such a toggle. (Pardon me whilst I swallow my pride for this next section title.)

Hail AlphaImageLoader, the conquering hero

Ever tried to get transparent PNGs working in IE6 and below? Chances are good you've encountered `AlphaImageLoader`, one of Microsoft's proprietary CSS filters (http://bkaprt.com/rwd2/15/). There have since been more robust patches created for IE's lack of support for the PNG alpha channel (Drew Diller's DD_belatedPNG library is an old favorite of mine: http://bkaprt.com/rwd2/16/), but historically, if you had a PNG attached to an element's background, you could drop the following rule into an IE-specific stylesheet:

```
.logo {
  background: none;
  filter: progid:DXImageTransform.Microsoft. »
    AlphaImageLoader(src="/path/to/logo.png", »
    sizingMethod="scale");
}
```

This `AlphaImageLoader` patch does a few things. First, it removes the background image from the element, then inserts it into an `AlphaImageLoader` object that sits "between" the proper background layer and the element's content. But the `sizingMethod` property (http://bkaprt.com/rwd2/17/) is the clever bit, dictating whether the `AlphaImageLoader` object should `crop` any parts of the image that overflow its container, treat it like a regular `image`, or `scale` it to fit it within its containing element.

I can hear you stifling your yawns by now: after all, what does an IE-specific PNG fix have to do with our broken image rendering? Quite a bit, as it turns out. At one point I discovered that applying `AlphaImageLoader` to an image dramatically improves its rendering quality in IE, bringing it up to par with, well, every other browser on the planet. Furthermore, by setting the `sizingMethod` property to scale, we can use our `AlphaImageLoader` object to create the illusion of a flexible image.

So I whipped up some JavaScript to automate that process. Simply download the script (available at http://bkaprt.com/rwd2/18/) and include it on any page with flexible images; it will scour your document to create a series of flexible, high-quality `AlphaImageLoader` objects.

And with that fix applied, the difference in our rendered images is noticeable (**FIG 3.8**): in our example we've gone from an impossibly distorted image to an immaculately rendered one. And it works wonderfully in a flexible context.

(It's worth mentioning that many of Microsoft's proprietary filters, and `AlphaImageLoader` in particular, have some performance overhead associated with them—Stoyan Stefanov covers the pitfalls in more detail on the YUI blog: http://bkaprt.com/rwd2/19/. What does this mean for you? Just be sure to test the fix thoroughly on your site, gauge its effect on your users, and evaluate whether or not the improved rendering is worth the performance tradeoff.)

With the `max-width: 100%` fix in place (and aided by our `width: 100%` and `AlphaImageLoader` patches), our inset image is resizing beautifully across our target browsers. No matter the

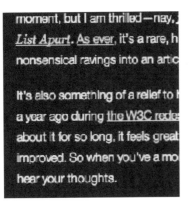

FIG 3.8: Our image is now perfectly legible, and resizing wonderfully. A dab of AlphaImageLoader'll do ya.

size of the browser window, our image scales harmoniously along with the proportions of our flexible grid.

But what about images that aren't actually in our markup?

FLEXIBLY TILED BACKGROUND IMAGES

Let's say our dearly esteemed designer sends over a revised mockup of our blog module. Notice anything different about it? (**FIG 3.9**)

Up until now, our blog's content has been sitting on a rather unassuming near-white background. But now the design has been modified slightly, adding a two-toned background to the blog entry to provide more contrast between the left- and right-hand columns. What's more, there's actually a subtle level of noise added to the background, adding an extra level of texture to our design (**FIG 3.10**).

So: how do we actually add this new background image to our template?

Back in 2004, Dan Cederholm wrote a brilliant article showing how a vertically repeating background graphic could be used to create a "faux column" effect (http://bkaprt.com/rwd2/20/). The technique's genius is in its simplicity: by tiling a colored

FIG 3.9: Our blog's sidebar is now sporting a background graphic. Hot.

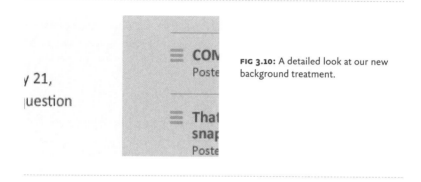

FIG 3.10: A detailed look at our new background treatment.

background graphic vertically behind our content, we can create the illusion of equal height columns.

In Dan's original technique, the background graphic was simply centered at the top of the content area and then tiled vertically, like so:

```
.blog {
    background: #F8F5F2 url("blog-bg.png") repeat-y 50% 0;
}
```

And that technique works beautifully. But Dan's technique assumes that your design is a fixed width, creating a graphic that matches the width of your design. Then how, pray, are we supposed to work in a background image that tiles over two *flexible* columns?

Thanks to some early research by designer Doug Bowman (http://bkaprt.com/rwd2/21/), we can still apply the faux column technique. It just requires a little bit of extra planning, as well as a dash of your favorite formula, target ÷ context = result.

First, we'll begin by taking a look at our mockup, to find the *transition point* in our background graphic, the exact pixel at which our white column transitions into the gray. And from the look of things, that switch happens at the 568 pixel mark (**FIG 3.11**). Armed with that information, we can now adapt the "faux columns" approach to our fluid grid. First, we'll convert that transition point into a percentage-based value relative to our blog module's width. And to do so, our target ÷ context = result formula comes into play yet again. We have our *target* value of 568px, and the width of the design—our *context*—is 900px. And if we plug those two values into our stalwart formula:

```
568 ÷ 900 = 0.631111111111111
```

That's right: another impossibly long number, which converts to a percentage of 63.1111111111111%.

Keep that percentage in the back of your mind for a moment. Now, let's open up your favorite image editor, and create a foolishly wide document—say, one that's 3000 pixels across (**FIG 3.12**). And since we're going to tile this image vertically, its height is only 160px tall.

In a moment, we're going to turn this blank document into our background graphic. But why is it so large? Well, this image needs to be larger than we can reasonably assume the browser window will ever be. And unless you're reading this from the 25th century on your wall-sized display made of, I don't know, holograms or whatever, I'm assuming your monitor's not *quite* that wide.

To create the columns themselves, we'll need to apply the transition point percentage (63.1111111111111%) to our new, wider canvas. So if we're working with a graphic that's 3000px across, we simply need to multiply that width by the percentage, like so:

900px   **568px**

"KILL ALL HUMANS?" BUT WHY?

The last question was asked for the first time, half in jest, on May 21,

≡ COMPLIANCE
Posted by Max on 23 Dec 2010

FIG 3.11: Our white column switches over to gray at the 568px mark. That's our transition point.

3000px

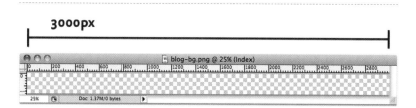

FIG 3.12: A monstrously large canvas that we'll (shortly) turn into our background graphic.

63.11111%
(or **1893px**)

3000px

FIG 3.13: We've applied that percentage to our oh-so-wide background graphic, creating our tile-ready columns.

```
3000 x 0.631111111111111 = 1893.333333333333
```

We're left with 1893.333333333333 as our result. And since Photoshop doesn't deal in anything less than whole pixels, let's round that down to 1893 pixels. Armed with that number, we'll recreate our textures in our blank image, switching from white to gray at the 1893rd pixel (**FIG 3.13**).

How does that help us? Well, what we've just done is to proportionally scale our transition point *up* to this new, wider canvas. So we can take that new pixel value, and use it to create our columns: the white column will be 1893px wide, with the gray column filling up the remainder.

So now there's only one thing left to do: drop our newly minted graphic into our stylesheet.

```
.blog {
    background: #F8F5F2 url("blog-bg.png") repeat-y   »
        63.1111111111111% 0;   /* 568px / 900px */
}
```

As in Dan's original technique, we're still positioning the graphic at the very top of our blog, and then repeating it vertically down the width of the module (repeat-y). But the background-position value reuses our transition point percentage (63.1111111111111% 0), keeping the columns firmly in place as our design resizes itself.

And with that, we've got faux columns working beautifully in a fluid layout (FIG 3.14). All thanks to Dan Cederholm's original approach, augmented with a little proportional thinking.

Fully flexible background images?

Of course, our flexible faux column isn't *really* flexible: we're simply using percentages to position a background image in such a way that the columns appear to resize with their container. The image's dimensions haven't changed at all.

But what about a background image that actually does need to resize with the layout? Perhaps you've placed a logo on an h1 element's background, or used sprites to create rollovers for your site's navigation. Can we resize images that *need* to live in the background?

Well, sort of. There is a CSS3 property called background-size (http://bkaprt.com/rwd2/22/), which would allow us to create truly flexible background images. Depending on your audience, browser support might be a little uneven, especially if you're supporting Internet Explorer 8.0 or lower.

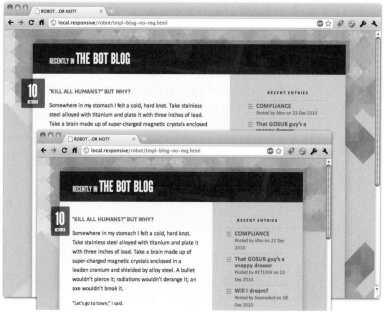

FIG 3.14: Our flexibly faux columns.

But all is not lost! There are some rather ingenious JavaScript-based solutions out there: for example, Modernizr (http://modernizr.com/) allows you to test if a browser supports certain CSS properties like background-size and, if not, serve appropriate fallback styles; alternately, Scott Robbin's jQuery Backstretch plugin (http://bkaprt.com/rwd2/23/) simulates resizable background images on the body element. And as you'll see in the next chapter, CSS3 media queries could also be used to apply different background images tailored to different resolution ranges. So while background-size might not work everywhere, the sky is still, as the kids say, the limit.

LEARNING TO LOVE OVERFLOW

There are a few other options for working fixed-width images into a fluid context. In fact, you might consider browsing through Richard Rutter's experiments with wide images placed in flexible layouts (http://bkaprt.com/rwd2/13/). There are a number of promising experiments listed there, some of which might prove useful to you as you start tinkering with flexible layouts. One method I've used on a few occasions is the `overflow` property. As we saw earlier in the chapter, wide images will, by default, simply bleed out of their containing elements. And in most cases, the `max-width: 100%` rule is the best way to constrain them, snapping them back down to a manageable size. But alternately, you could simply clip off that excess image data by applying `overflow: hidden`. So rather than setting our inset image to resize itself automatically...

```
.feature img {
  max-width: 100%;
}
```

...we could instead simply clip off all that excess, overflowing data like so:

```
.feature {
  overflow: hidden;
}

.feature img {
  display: block;
  max-width: auto;
}
```

And there you have it: one image, cropped to fit inside its container (**FIG 3.15**). The image is all still there, but the excess bits have just been hidden from view.

Now, as you can see, this isn't really a *workable* solution. In fact, I've found that in the overwhelming majority of cases, `overflow` is generally less useful than scaling the image via `max-width`. But still, it's an option to consider, and one you might find some use for.

"Coming?" I asked.

Jack was pale under his freckles but Chief Dalton grinned back at me. "We'll be right behind you, Morrison," he said.

Behind me! So they could pick up the pieces. I gave them a cocky smile and switched on the engine, full speed.

Carron City is about a mile from the plant. It has about fifty thousand inhabitants. At that moment, though, there wasn't a soul in the streets. I heard people calling to each other inside their houses, but I didn't see anyone, human or android. I circled in for a landing, the Police Copter hovering maybe a quarter of a mile back of me. Then, as the wheels touched, half a dozen androids came around the corner. They saw me and

Lo, the robot walks

FIG 3.15: And with a dash of overflow: hidden applied to our image's container, we're left with an image that's…well, cropped. Yay, I guess?

NEGOTIATE THAT CONTENT

It's worth noting that both the overflow and max-width: 100% approaches to flexible images are actually pretty robust, and work remarkably well for most kinds of media. In fact, I've used them successfully on a number of complex fluid grids.

However, both approaches are ultimately "content-blind." Each establishes some basic rules for the way an image interacts with its container: max-width: 100% scales oversized images down to match the width of their containers, while controlling overflow allows the designer to conceal any image data that might bleed out of its containing element.

But what about especially complex graphics? If your image is especially information-rich (**FIG 3.16**), simply scaling or cropping it might be less than desirable—in fact, those approaches might actually *impede* your readers' ability to understand the content contained in that image.

If that's the case, it might be worth investigating ways of delivering different versions of the same image to different resolution ranges. In other words, you could create multiple versions of your infographic—say, one ideal for desktop browsers, as well as another, more linearized version for small-screen devices. With those options established, a server-side solution could intelligently serve the most appropriate image for that resolution range.

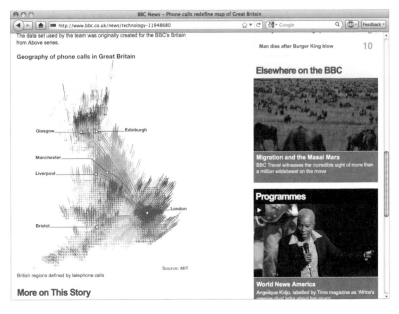

FIG 3.16: This rich infographic from the BBC News site (http://bkaprt.com/rwd2/24/) contains information critical to the page's content. Simply scaling it down could prove counterproductive.

Creating such a solution is beyond the scope of this book (and beyond the skill of your humble author), but there's good news: a `picture` element is in the process of coming to HTML, one that would allow us to load images responsively, switching in different graphics depending on certain conditions in the browser—say, the width of the viewport:

```
<picture>
  <source srcset="img/large.jpg" media="(min-width: »
    800px)">
  <source srcset="img/default.jpg">
  <img srcset="img/default.jpg" alt="A gray cat looks »
    on with anticipation">
</picture>
```

FIG 3.17: Two chapters later, and we've finally got a completed grid-based layout that can expand and contract with a changing viewport.

In the above code, we're using `picture` to conditionally serve different images via two `source` elements inside it: specifically, a small-screen-friendly `default.jpg` is shown unless the screen is at least `800px` wide, at which point `large.jpg` is shown instead. (Wondering about those `media` attributes? We'll cover media *queries* in the next chapter.)

Now, the `picture` element is still in the process of being standardized, with browser implementations expected to arrive soon, but the Picturefill JavaScript library (http://bkaprt.com/ rwd2/25/) allows you to use `picture` *today.* Which is great! But what's more, there are myriad ways of serving different images in a responsive context—many of them client-side, some requiring some server-side code. (For a comprehensive look at some of the best approaches, I heartily recommend Scott Jehl's *Responsible Responsive Design,* available via A Book Apart.)

But regardless of *how* you decide to conditionally load your images, your approach could be augmented by the various client-side techniques we've discussed so far. For example, you could serve images to a limited number of resolutions, and then use `max-width: 100%` to smooth the transition to other devices, browsers, and resolution ranges on an as-needed basis.

FLEXIBLE GRIDS AND IMAGES, UP IN THE PROVERBIAL TREE

At this point, we've explored everything you need to build complex but flexible grid-based layouts: the simple math behind flexible grids, and some strategies for working images and other media into that framework. While we've been focusing on building a fairly simple blog module, we can actually use this to build the rest of the Robot or Not site, creating a design that's founded on a system of proportions and percentages, with nary a pixel in sight (**FIG 3.17**).

With this flexible foundation in place, we're ready to add the final ingredient to our responsive design.

(And no, it's not mixed metaphors.)

4 MEDIA QUERIES

FOR MOST of my career, I've been a staunch proponent of non-fixed layouts. Flexible or completely fluid, it didn't matter: I felt that building *some* measure of fluidity into our designs better prepared them for the changes inherent to the web: changes in the user's browser window size, in display or device resolution. What's more, I'd often use words like "future-proof" and "device-agnostic" when describing the need for this flexibility. Often while standing alone at parties.

But at some point, everything breaks.

As flexible as the Robot site is right now, it's not completely bulletproof. Sure, its fluid grid makes it pretty resilient to changes in window size and screen resolution—much more so than a fixed layout would. But even slight changes to the size and shape of the browser window will cause our layout to warp, bend, and possibly break outright.

Here's the thing, though: that's okay.

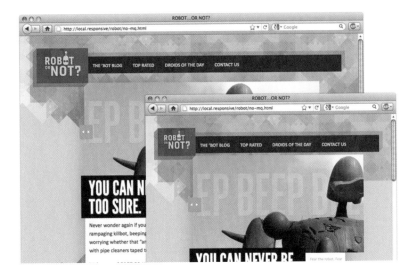

FIG 4.1: By adjusting the size of our browser window, we can get a quick sense of how our design performs at different resolutions.

LET THE HEALING BEGIN

As painful as it might be, let's look at some of the areas where our design breaks as it reshapes itself. By identifying the problems we're facing, we'll be in a better position to apply the needed fixes. Even if we shed a tear or three in the process.

Since we're working with a flexible layout, we can simply resize the browser window to a few different widths. Now, this is no substitute for actually testing our work on separate devices. But it allows us to quickly assess how our design handles several different resolution ranges, and simulate how users on capable phones, tablets, or other devices might experience our design.

A question of emphasis

Let's begin by bringing the browser window in a bit, from around 1024 pixels wide to roughly 760 pixels or so (FIG 4.1). Pretty quickly, a number of problems appear.

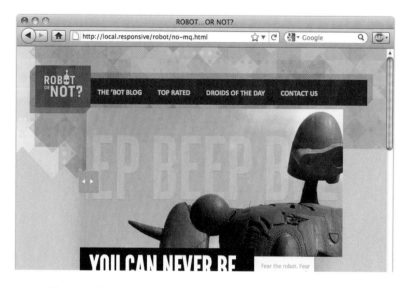

FIG 4.2: It's not exactly sunshine and puppies at the top of our design. Whatever *that* means.

Our initial design was all about emphasis: large, imposing headlines, a prominent lead image, and generous margins. All of which still scale inside our flexible layout—but visually speaking, the priorities have gone way off.

Look at the top of our site, where the lead image now dominates the entire page (FIG 4.2). Since we're cropping the image with the `overflow` property, it isn't scaling with the rest of our flexible grid. What's more, the subject of the image, our beloved robot, is actually getting pretty severely clipped. So we're left with an image that's not only huge, but barely comprehensible. Fantastic.

Sitting in the shadow of that gigantic graphic, our logo has scaled down to a nearly microscopic size. And what little padding we enjoyed between the navigation and the lead image has been lost, making the entire masthead feel claustrophobic.

As much as I hate to say it, our visual hierarchy is reduced to shambles as soon as we move slightly below the resolution we originally designed for.

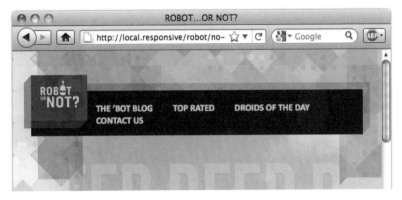

FIG 4.3: Every visitor to our site will absolutely love this broken-looking navigation. No, trust me. They totally will.

Miniature grid, monster problems

And that's not the worst of it. If we bring the browser window in a bit more to around 600 pixels—the width of a small browser window, or of newer tablet computers held in portrait mode—the headaches just keep coming (**FIG 4.3**). At the top of the screen, our visual hierarchy's still a mess: the lead image is now cropped to the point of incoherence, and our poor logo is even more of a thumbnail. But now our primary navigation is wrapping in a fairly embarrassing manner. Surely we can do better than that?

Moving down the page, our blog is really starting to suffer (**FIG 4.4**). Where the two-column layout once provided easy access to some additional information, it now makes content in each column feel constricted. In particular, the article's lines are uncomfortably short, making for a decidedly awful reading experience. And the photo set within our blog entry looks inconsequential, the content of the picture almost hard to discern.

Finally, to conclude our little sideshow of tears, the photo module at the bottom of the page is probably the worst of all (**FIG 4.5**). You thought the image in our blog entry was bad? These photos are comically small, and nearly indecipherable.

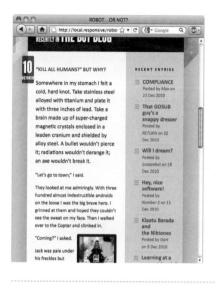

FIG 4.4: Reading this entry / feels like scanning a haiku: / painfully short lines.

FIG 4.5: Tiny pictures, monstrous margins. A match made in...well, somewhere not great.

The generous margins we initially used to frame those pictures now seem wildly out of proportion, drowning our photos in a sea of white space.

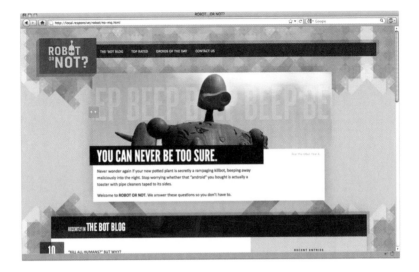

FIG 4.6: That intro is just uncomfortably wide.

Widescreen woes

Our problems aren't isolated to the smaller end of the resolution spectrum, however. If we maximize our browser window, a whole new slew of design issues present themselves.

The intro (**FIG 4.6**) doesn't look awful, but the image is now smaller than the space allotted for it. That aside, things don't look terrible up top—far from ideal, I admit, but not utterly abysmal either. In general, our flexible grid looks okay up there.

So let's quash those good feelings by scrolling down to look at the blog (**FIG 4.7**). Remember how clipped our entry's lines felt in the smaller window? I'm almost missing those cramped spaces, because *these* lines are just frighteningly long: the width of that article column is entirely too generous at this level. As much as my eye loves to spend hours circling back to the beginning of the next line I'm supposed to read, there has to be a better way.

And finally, our photo gallery completely dominates the bottom of the page (**FIG 4.8**). The images themselves look fine, but

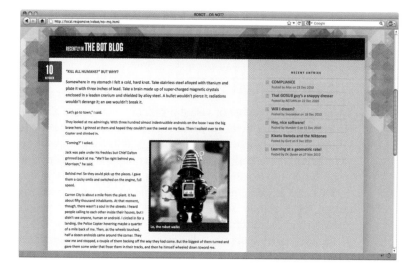

FIG 4.7: Moving down the page, the blog doesn't fare quite so well. Long lines, tiny images, sad Ethan.

FIG 4.8: These images are, to use a technical term, large 'n' chunky.

they're cartoonishly large. In fact, on my monitor there's no hint of any content above or below the module. Is this really the best way to present this information to our readers?

THE PROBLEM AT HAND

We've identified a host of visual problems. But there's a larger issue coming into focus. As we move beyond the resolution for which it was originally designed, our grid becomes a liability to our content. Its proportions constrict our content at smaller resolutions, and isolate it in a sea of white space at higher ones.

This isn't a problem unique to flexible layouts, however. No design, fixed or fluid, scales well beyond the context for which it was originally designed.

So how can we create a design that can adapt to changes in screen resolution and viewport dimensions? How can our page optimize itself for the myriad browsers and devices that access it?

In other words, how can our designs become more *responsive?*

SLOUCHING TOWARD RESPONSIVENESS

Thankfully, the W3C has been wrestling with this question for some time. To better understand the solution they eventually presented, it's worth reviewing a bit of the backstory.

Meet the media types

Their first stab at a solution was media types, part of the CSS2 specification (http://bkaprt.com/rwd2/26/). Here's how they were first described:

> On occasion, however, style sheets for different media types may share a property, but require different values for that property. For example, the "font-size" property is useful both for screen and print media. The two media types are different enough to

require different values for the common property; a document will typically need a larger font on a computer screen than on paper. Therefore, it is necessary to express that a style sheet, or a section of a style sheet, applies to certain media types.

Okay, yeah. That's a bit obtuse, isn't it? Let's try it in non-robot terms.

Ever written a print stylesheet (http://bkaprt.com/rwd2/27/)? Then you're already familiar with the concept of designing for different *kinds* of media. The ideal browsing experience couldn't differ more between desktop browsers and printers, or between handheld devices and speaking browsers. To address this the W3C created a list of *media types* (http://bkaprt.com/ rwd2/28/), attempting to classify each browser or device under a broad, media-specific category. The recognized media types are: all, braille, embossed, handheld, print, projection, screen, speech, tty, and tv.

Some of these media types, like print or screen, or perhaps even projection, are probably ones you've used before. Perhaps others like embossed (for paged braille printers) or speech (for speaking browsers and interfaces) seem new. But all of these media types were created so that we could better design for each *type* of browser or device, by conditionally loading CSS tailored for each. So a screen-based device would ignore CSS loaded with the print media type, and vice versa. And for style rules meant to apply to all devices, the specification created the all supergroup.

In practice, that meant customizing the media attribute of a link:

```
<link rel="stylesheet" href="global.css" media="all" />
<link rel="stylesheet" href="main.css" media="screen" />
<link rel="stylesheet" href="paper.css" media="print" />
```

Or perhaps creating an @media block in your stylesheet, and associating it with a particular media type:

```
@media screen {
  body {
    font-size: 100%;
  }
}

@media print {
  body {
    font-size: 15pt;
  }
}
```

In each case, the specification suggests the browser would identify itself as belonging to one of the media types. ("I'm a desktop browser! I belong to the screen media type." "I smell like ink cartridges and toner: I'm print media." "I'm your video game console's browser: I'm media tv." And so on.) Upon loading the page, the browser would then render only the CSS pertaining to its particular media type, and disregard the rest. And in theory, this is a fantastic idea.

Theory being, of course, the last thing hard-working web designers need.

Miscast types

Several problems with media types became evident when all these little small-screen browsers, like phones and tablets, arrived on the scene. According to the specification, designers could have targeted them simply by creating a stylesheet for the handheld media type:

```
<link rel="stylesheet" href="main.css" media="screen" />
<link rel="stylesheet" href="paper.css" media="print" />
<link rel="stylesheet" href="tiny.css" »
  media="handheld"/>
```

The problem with this approach is, well, us—at least in part. Early mobile devices didn't have sufficiently capable browsers so we largely ignored them, choosing instead to design compelling screen- or print-specific stylesheets. And when capable small-screen browsers finally *did* appear, there weren't a lot of handheld CSS files scattered about the web. As a result, many mobile browser makers decided to default to reading screen-based stylesheets.

But what's more, media types paint with an incredibly broad brush. Is one handheld stylesheet really suited to address the challenges of designing for an iPhone *and* a five year-old feature phone?

Enter the media query

Realizing some of the failings of media types, the W3C used their work on CSS3 to take another crack at the problem. The result was **media queries** (http://bkaprt.com/rwd2/29/), an incredibly robust mechanism for identifying not only types of media, but for actually inspecting the physical characteristics of the devices and browsers that render our content.

Let's take a look:

```
@media screen and (min-width: 1024px) {
  body {
    font-size: 100%;
  }
}
```

Now, every media query—including the one above—has two components:

1. Each query still begins with a media **type** (screen), drawn from the CSS2.1 specification's list of approved media types (http://bkaprt.com/rwd2/28/).
2. Immediately after comes the **query** itself, wrapped in parentheses: (min-width: 1024px). And our query can, in turn, be split into two components: the name of a **feature** (min-width) and a corresponding **value** (1024px).

Think of a media query like a test for your browser. When a browser reads your stylesheet, the `screen and (min-width: 1024px)` query asks two questions: first, if it belongs to the `screen` media type; and if it does, if the browser's viewport is at least 1024 pixels wide. If the browser meets both of those criteria, then the styles enclosed within the query are rendered; if not, the browser happily disregards the styles, and continues on its merry way.

Our media query above is written as part of an `@media` declaration, which enables us to put queries directly inside a stylesheet. But you can also place queries on `link` elements by inserting them into the `media` attribute:

```
<link rel="stylesheet" href="wide.css" media="screen »
    and (min-width: 1024px)" />
```

Or you can attach them to `@import` statements:

```
@import url("wide.css") screen and (min-width: 1024px);
```

I personally prefer the `@media` approach since it keeps your code consolidated in a single file, while reducing the number of extraneous requests the browser has to make to your server.

But no matter how you write your queries, the result in each scenario is the same: if the browser matches the media type *and* meets the condition outlined in our query, it applies the enclosed CSS. Otherwise, it won't.

Meet the features

It's not just about testing for width and height. There are a host of features listed in the specification our queries can test. But before we dive in, it's worth noting that the language used to describe the features can be a bit...dense. Here are two quick guidelines that helped me sort it out:

1. In the spec's language, every device has a "display area" and "rendering surface." Clear as mud, that. But think of it this way: the browser's viewport is the display area; the entire

display is the rendering surface. So on your laptop, the display area would be your browser window; the rendering surface would be your screen. (I don't makes the terms. I just explains 'em.)

2. To test values above or below a certain threshold, some features accept `min-` and `max-` prefixes. A fine example is `width`: you can serve CSS conditionally to viewports above 1024 pixels by writing (`min-width: 1024px`), or below 1024 pixels with (`max-width: 1024px`).

Got all that? Fantastic. With those two points out of the way, let's dive into the features the specification says we can use in our queries (http://bkaprt.com/rwd2/30/) (**TABLE 4.1**).

What's *really* exciting is that we can chain multiple queries together with the `and` keyword:

```
@media screen and (min-device-width: 480px) and »
  (orientation: landscape) { … }
```

This allows us to test for multiple features in a single query, creating more complex tests for the devices viewing our designs.

Know thy features

Feeling drunk with power yet? Well, I should take this opportunity to mention that not all @media-aware browsers support querying for all features outlined in the specification.

Here's a quick example: when Apple's iPad first launched, it shipped with media query support for `orientation`. That meant you could write `orientation: landscape` or `orientation: portrait` queries to conditionally serve up CSS to the device, depending on how it was being held. Cool, no? Sadly, the iPhone didn't support the `orientation` query until an OS upgrade arrived a few months later. While each device allowed the user to change its orientation, the iPhone's browser didn't understand the queries for that particular feature.

The moral of this story? Research your target devices and browsers thoroughly for the query features they do support, and test accordingly.

FEATURE NAME	DEFINITION	HAS min- AND max- PREFIXES
width	The width of the display area.	✔
height	The height of the display area.	✔
device-width	The width of the device's rendering surface.	✔
device-height	The height of the device's rendering surface.	✔
orientation	Accepts portrait or landscape values.	✘
aspect-ratio	Ratio of the display area's width over its height. For example: on a desktop, you'd be able to query if the browser window is at a 16:9 aspect ratio.	✔
device-aspect-ratio	Ratio of the device's rendering surface width over its height. For example: on a desktop, you'd be able to query if the screen is at a 16:9 aspect ratio.	✔
color	The number of bits per color component of the device. For example, an 8-bit color device would successfully pass a query of (color: 8). Non-color devices should return a value of 0.	✔
color-index	The number of entries in the color lookup table of the output device. For example, @ media screen and (min-color-index: 256).	✔

FEATURE NAME	DEFINITION	HAS min- AND max- PREFIXES
monochrome	Similar to color, the monochrome feature lets us test the number of bits per pixel in a monochrome device.	✔
resolution	Tests the density of the pixels in the device, such as screen and (resolution: 72dpi) or screen and (max-resolution: 300dpi).	✔
scan	For tv-based browsing, measures whether the scanning process is either progressive or scan.	✘
scan	Tests whether the device is a grid-based display, like feature phones with one fixed-width font. Can be expressed simply as (grid).	✘

TABLE 4.1: A list of the device features we can test in our media queries.

But while support may still be developing among modern browsers and devices, media queries already give us an incredibly broad vocabulary, one we can use to articulate how we'd like our designs to appear in various devices and browsers.

A MORE RESPONSIVE ROBOT

And this is why media queries are the final component of a responsive website. We've spent two chapters implementing our flexible, grid-based layout—but this is only our foundation. As that layout scales up or down, we can use media queries to correct any visual imperfections that crop up as the viewport reshapes itself.

What's more, we can use media queries to optimize the display of our content to best meet the needs of the device, creating alternate layouts tailored to different resolution ranges. By conditionally loading style rules that target these ranges, media queries allow us to create pages that are more sensitive to the needs of the devices that render them.

In other words, by combining flexible layouts and media queries, we'll finally be able to make our sites *responsive.*

Let's get started.

A room with a viewport

We've already identified a number of stress points in our design. But before we start applying our media queries, we need to make one final tweak to our markup.

When Apple launched the iPhone in 2007, they created a new attribute value for Mobile Safari's `meta` element: `viewport` (http://bkaprt.com/rwd2/31/). Why? Well, the dimensions of the iPhone's display is 320×480, but Mobile Safari actually displays web pages at a width of 980 pixels. If you've ever visited Apple's homepage (http://apple.com/) on a WebKit-enabled phone (**FIG 4.9**), then you've seen this behavior in action: Mobile Safari is drawing the page upon a `980px`-wide canvas, and then shrinking it to fit within your phone's 320×480 display.

Using the `viewport` tag allows us to control the size of that canvas, and override that default behavior: we can dictate exactly how wide the browser's viewport should be. For example, we could set our pages at a fixed width of `320px`:

```
<meta name="viewport" content="width=320" />
```

Since being introduced by Apple, a number of mobile browser makers have adopted the `viewport` mechanic, creating something of a *de facto* standard. So let's incorporate it into our soon-to-be responsive design. But instead of declaring a fixed pixel

FIG 4.9: By default, Mobile Safari renders web content at 980px wide— even though its display is 320px wide when held in portrait mode.

width, we're going to take a more resolution-agnostic approach. In the head of our HTML, let's drop in this meta element:

```
<meta name="viewport" content="initial-scale=1.0, »
    width=device-width" />
```

The initial-scale property sets the zoom level of the page to 1.0, or 100%, and helps ensure some consistency across small-screen, viewport-aware browsers. (For more information on

FIG 4.10: Here's our high-impact headline treatment, looking all impactful.

YOU CAN NEVER BE TOO SURE.

Never wonder again if your new potted plant is secretly a ran

how scaling works on different displays, I recommend Mozilla's explanation: http://bkaprt.com/rwd2/32/.)

But the important bit for us is the `width=device-width` setting, which makes the width of the browser's viewport equal to the width of the device's screen. So on an iPhone, for example, Mobile Safari's layout area wouldn't default to `980px` anymore. Instead, it would be 320 pixels wide in portrait mode; in landscape, 480 pixels wide.

With this value in place, we can use `max-width` and `min-width` to look for resolution ranges below or above certain resolution thresholds, and conditionally load in CSS designed for those ranges. What's more, this allows all query-aware browsers to take advantage of our media queries, making the design responsive for all users—whether they're using phones, tablets, desktop computers, or laptops.

Okay, enough of my jabbering. Let's see this in action.

MEDIA QUERIES IN ACTION

Remember those large, imposing headlines (**FIG 4.10**)? Well, here's the CSS that currently styles them:

```
.main-title {
  background: #000;
  color: #FFF;
  font: normal 3.625em/0.9 "League Gothic", "Arial »
    Narrow", Arial, sans-serif;  /* 58px / 16px */
  text-transform: uppercase;
}
```

I've left out a few presentational properties, because what I'm most concerned about is just how stupidly huge those headlines are at smaller resolutions. They're set in the stately League Gothic (http://bkaprt.com/rwd2/33/), colored in white (color: #FFF) on a black background (background: #000). And in case there was any doubt that these headlines were meant to be taken *very seriously*, they're displayed in uppercase through a dash of text-transform, and then sized at an imposing 3.625em, or 58px.

Now, that treatment works well enough. But as we've just seen, it doesn't look great once we've less real estate to work with. Whether viewed in narrower browser windows or on smaller device displays, that design just doesn't scale.

So let's fix that.

First, we'll create an @media block somewhere after our initial .main-title rule, one that queries for a narrower resolution range:

```
@media screen and (max-width: 768px) { … }
```

In this query, we've asked that the browser render the enclosed CSS *only if* its viewport is no wider than 768 pixels. Why 768px? Well, media query-aware phones, as well as most recent tablets, fall well beneath this threshold. Or at least, they do when held a certain way: for example, the iPad's resolution is 768px across when held in portrait mode, but 1024px when held in landscape mode.

But since we're using max-width, not max-device-width, narrower browser windows on your desktop or laptop will apply this small-screen-friendly range as well. (Remember: width and height measure the viewport or browser window, whereas device-width and device-height measure the dimensions of the entire screen.)

With this query in place, we can start targeting the elements of our design that don't scale down that well. Let's begin by rethinking our oversized headline treatment. To do so, we'll place a .main-title rule inside our media query, overwriting the CSS properties that are causing us headaches:

```
@media screen and (max-width: 768px) {
  .main-title {
    font: normal 1.5em Calibri, Candara, Segoe, »
      "Segoe UI", Optima, Arial, Helvetica, »
      sans-serif;  /* 24px / 16px */
  }
}
```

Our first `.main-title` rule is still applied by all browsers reading our CSS. But for narrower browser windows and devices—specifically, those no wider than 768 pixels—the second rule is applied as well, overriding its predecessor. We've made two changes of note here: first, we've set a smaller font size on the `.main-title` element, changing it from `3.625em` (roughly `58px`) to a much smaller `1.5em`, or `24px`, that feels more appropriate on smaller displays.

Secondly, the typeface we were initially using for our headlines—our beloved League Gothic—doesn't scale down very well to that size (**FIG 4.11**). So I've decided to change the `font-family` stack itself (`Calibri, Candara, Segoe, "Segoe UI", Optima, Arial, Helvetica, sans-serif`), which feels a bit more readable (**FIG 4.12**).

Now, you've probably noticed that we didn't have to rewrite the other properties from the first `.main-title` rule. As a result, the black background color, all-caps `text-transform`, and white color still apply to our miniaturized headlines. Our query only overwrites the features we don't want.

And presto: by quickly applying a media query, we've whipped up a headline treatment that feels much more appropriate for smaller displays (**FIG 4.13**).

But this is just the beginning. Not only can we fine-tune our typography to respond to changes in resolution, we can also tackle our larger design problems as well.

Thinking in miniature

In fact, let's begin by building on our new media query, and make a slight change to our page's layout. Remember our flexible `.page` container from Chapter 2? Here's what its CSS currently looks like:

YOU CAN NEVER BE TOO SURE.

Never wonder again if your new potte
killbot, beeping away maliciously into t
that "android" you bought is actually a

FIG 4.11: League Gothic, lovely though it is, shines best as display copy. But here, it's a little too tiny.

YOU CAN NEVER BE TOO SURE.

Never wonder again if your new potted plant is secretl
killbot, beeping away maliciously into the night. Stop w
that "android" you bought is actually a toaster with nu

FIG 4.12: Less sexy than League Gothic? Most things are. Still, it's much more legible, and works with the design.

YOU CAN NEVER BE TOO SURE.

Fear t

Never wonder again if your new potted plant is

FIG 4.13: Our default headline view above, with the media query-corrected version below.

YOU CAN NEVER BE TOO SURE.

Fear t

Never wonder again if your new potted plant is
secretly a rampaging killbot, beeping away
maliciously into the night. Stop worrying whether

```
.page {
  margin: 36px auto;
  width: 90%;
}
```

Our container's currently set to 90% of the browser window, and centered horizontally (margin: 36px auto). Works great, but let's add a rule inside our existing media query to tweak its behavior once we start falling below our initial resolution:

```
@media screen and (max-width: 768px) {
  .page {
    position: relative;
    margin: 20px;
    width: auto;
  }
}
```

Below 768px, we're instructing the .page element to occupy the full width of the browser window, save for a fixed 20px-wide margin around its edges. A minor change, but this will afford us a bit more space at smaller screen resolutions.

With our container sorted, we can turn our attention to the content area.

```
@media screen and (max-width: 768px) {
  .page {
    margin: 20px;
    width: auto;
  }

  .welcome,
  .blog,
  .gallery {
    margin: 0 0 30px;
    width: auto;
  }
}
```

This new rule selects the three top-level content modules—our introduction (.welcome), the blog (.blog), and photo gallery (.gallery)—and disables their horizontal margins, making them occupy the full width of .page.

And just like that, we've linearized our page's layout, making it prime for reading on a smaller screen (**FIG 4.14**). Can I get a high five?

...No? What's that, you say? There's still a freakishly oversized image at the top of our page? (**FIG 4.15**)

Well, okay. I *suppose* we can clean that up. If it's really bothering you, I mean. But before we do, it's probably worth taking a quick look at the markup for that lead image, designed to be part of a (yet-to-be-implemented) slideshow module.

```
<div class="welcome section">
  <div class="slides">
    <div class="figure">
      <b><img src="img/slide-robot.jpg" alt="" /></b>
      <div class="figcaption">…</div>
    </div><!-- /end .figure -->

    <ul class="carousel-nav">
      <li><a class="prev" href="#">Previous</a></li>
      <li><a class="next" href="#">Next</a></li>
    </ul>
  </div><!-- /end .slides -->

  <div class="main">
    <h1 class="main-title">You can never be »
    too sure.</h1>
  </div><!-- /end .main -->
</div><!-- /end .welcome.section -->
```

There's a fair bit of HTML here, but basically we've created a .welcome module to contain our image as well as the introductory text that follows it (.main). Our image is part of a .figure block, with the img itself wrapped in a b element, which will act as a kind of "hook" for our CSS.

FIG 4.14: Our content's been linearized with two extra rules. Neat! But there's something amiss…

FIG 4.15: …specifically, that intro image still needs work.

Feel a bit crufty to you? I can see where you're coming from. But that b element, silly though it might appear, actually handles a fair bit of layout for us. Here's the relevant CSS:

```
.slides .figure b {
  display: block;
  overflow: hidden;
  margin-bottom: 0;
  width: 112.272727%;  /* 741px / 660px */
}
.slides .figure b img {
  display: block;
  max-width: inherit;
}
```

First, we've set `overflow` to `hidden` on the `b` element, creating a container that will crop any oversized content. But currently, our flexible images will simply resize themselves as the `b` element does, preventing that nice crop effect. So we've disabled the `max-width: 100%` scaling on our slideshow images (`max-width: inherit`). As a result, our big robot picture will simply get cropped if it's wider than the `b` element that contains it.

You might have noticed that the width of our `b` element is actually larger than 100%. We've used our old `target ÷ context = result` formula to create an element *larger* than the .welcome module, allowing the enclosed image to extend a bit off to the right.

But as my luck would have it, none of these effects work especially well at lower resolutions. (Related: I have awful luck.) So let's add a bit more to the end of our media query:

```
@media screen and (max-width: 768px) {
  .slides .figure b {
    width: auto;
  }

  .slides .figure b img {
    max-width: 100%;
  }
}
```

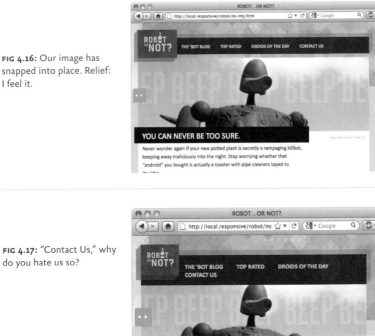

FIG 4.16: Our image has snapped into place. Relief: I feel it.

FIG 4.17: "Contact Us," why do you hate us so?

The first rule sets the `width` of our `b` container to `auto`, making it the same width as its container. The second rule actually reinstates the `max-width: 100%` behavior we discussed in Chapter 3, once again making the image expand and contract as its container does. Taken together, these two simple little rules do quite a bit, bringing our unruly image back in line with its container and, by extension, the rest of our design (**FIG 4.16**). I don't know about you, but I'm already breathing a sigh of relief.

Still, there's one more item we should tend to before putting our feet up. See our navigation up top? It's still feeling incredibly cramped. What's more, if we bring our viewport in even slightly, some decidedly un-awesome wrapping starts to occur (**FIG 4.17**).

The masthead markup is fairly straightforward:

```
<h1 class="logo">
  <a href="/">
    <i><img src="logo.png" alt="Robot or Not?" /></i>
  </a>
</h1>

<ul class="nav nav-primary">
  <li id="nav-blog"><a href="#">The &#8217;Bot Blog</a>
    </li>
  <li id="nav-rated"><a href="#">Top Rated</a></li>
  <li id="nav-droids"><a href="#">Droids of the Day</a>
    </li>
  <li id="nav-contact"><a href="#">Contact Us</a></li>
</ul><!-- /end ul.nav.nav-primary -->
```

That's right: we've marked up our logo with an `h1`, and an unordered list for the navigation. And, continuing in my oh-so-imaginative streak, they've been classed as `.logo` and `.nav-primary`, respectively. But what about the CSS?

```
.logo {
  background: #C52618 url("logo-bg.jpg");
  float: left;
  width: 16.875%;  /* 162px / 960px */
}

.nav-primary {
  background: #5E140D url("nav-bg.jpg");
  padding: 1.2em 1em 1em;
}

.nav-primary li {
  display: inline;
}
```

The styles are fairly modest. We're applying background images to both elements, but there's not much to the layout itself: we're floating the image to the left, causing it to overlap the navigation. And the individual list items inside our .nav-primary list are simply set to `display: inline`. Still, it works—at least until our page becomes narrow enough to cause our inline elements to wrap.

Into a media query we go:

```
@media screen and (max-width: 768px) {
  .logo {
    float: none;
    margin: 0 auto 20px;
    position: relative;
  }

  .nav-primary {
    margin-bottom: 20px;
    text-align: center;
  }
}
```

What we've done is to disable the `float` we'd initially set on our .logo, and instead centered it horizontally above our menu. And .nav-primary has been set to `text-align: center`, which centers our navigation items within it. Now as modifications go, these are pretty minor—the change, however, is fairly noticeable (**FIG 4.18**). Both the logo and our primary navigation are isolated on their own rows, with the proper priority accorded to each.

Personally, I'm pretty pleased with the way this looks—but we're not in the clear yet. Glancing over at the navigation, it looks like things are fairly tight at the moment: there's just not a lot of space left for our navigation items. In fact, if we bring in our screen by even a tiny amount, we're again facing some unseemly line wrapping (**FIG 4.19**).

(I appear to be on some sort of personal crusade against wrapping text. I don't know why.)

We've uncovered another breaking point, one that isn't fixed by simply moving the logo up to its own row. So let's create another media query, one primed to deal with just this contingency:

FIG 4.18: We can dramatically reorient the masthead at smaller resolutions, giving both our logo and the navigation a bit more room to breathe.

```
@media screen and (max-width: 768px) {
  ...
}

@media screen and (max-width: 520px) {
  .nav-primary {
    float: left;
    width: 100%;
  }
  .nav-primary li {
    clear: left;
    float: left;
    width: 48%;
  }

  li#nav-rated,
  li#nav-contact {
    clear: right;
    float: right;
  }

  .nav-primary a {
    display: block;
    padding: 0.45em;
  }
}
```

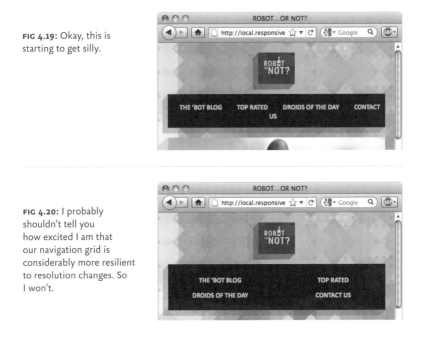

FIG 4.19: Okay, this is starting to get silly.

FIG 4.20: I probably shouldn't tell you how excited I am that our navigation grid is considerably more resilient to resolution changes. So I won't.

For even smaller screens—specifically, those narrower than 520 pixels—we've floated each `li` inside of `.nav-primary`, choosing to `float: right` the second and fourth menu items. The end result is a two-by-two grid of our navigation items, one that's more resilient to changes in viewport size than our display: inline approach (**FIG 4.20**).

It's worth pointing out that we didn't have to rewrite any of the rules from our previous query (`screen and (max-width: 768px)`) in this one. That's because screens that meet our new "narrower than `520px`" requirement *also* meet the "narrower than `768px`" requirement. In other words, rules from both queries are applied at the smallest end of the resolution spectrum. As a result, our second query only needs to concern itself with the design problems unique to viewports no wider than `520px`.

FIG 4.21: Our responsive design is shaping up beautifully, scaling on—and beyond—the desktop.

And there we are (**FIG 4.21**). With some additional tweaking to the internals of our page, we've finally got a design that *responds* to the context it's viewed in. We're no longer locked in to the grid, layout, or type we originally designed for one specific resolution range. When layered on top of our flexible layout, media queries allow us to address the design problems that result from those shrinking viewports.

This layout goes to eleven

But responsive web design isn't just about making designs accessible to smaller screens. You might recall that our design had a significant number of issues when it was viewed in a maximized browser window: images grew to unseemly sizes while lines of text became uncomfortably long, our grid stretched beyond the limits of usefulness (**FIGS 4.6-4.8**). Now, we *could* impose some sort of outer limit on our design, perhaps with a max-width set in ems or pixels. But let's instead treat this as an opportunity to design for another resolution range.

First, we'll begin by introducing another media query to do just that:

```
@media screen and (max-width: 768px) {

    ...

}

@media screen and (max-width: 520px) {

    ...

}

@media screen and (min-width: 1200px) {

    ...

}
```

Our first media query set a resolution ceiling of 768 pixels: in other words, devices and browser windows wider than that max-width limit would simply ignore the enclosed CSS. We quickly followed that up with another query for an even narrower range of 520px, once again using max-width to do so.

For our next query, we're instead using min-width to set 1200px as a baseline width requirement for all incoming browsers and devices. If they're wider than 1200 pixels, then they'll apply the enclosed styles; otherwise, they'll simply ignore the CSS, and go blithely about their business.

So let's roll up our sleeves and set to work on a widescreen-friendly layout:

```
@media screen and (min-width: 1200px) {
  .welcome,
  .blog,
  .gallery {
    width: 49.375%;
  }

  .welcome,
  .gallery {
    float: right;
    margin: 0 0 40px;
  }

  .blog {
    float: left;
    margin: 0 0 20px;
  }
}
```

In the live Robot site (http://responsivewebdesign.com/robot/),
you'll see a bunch of other changes that occur on this widescreen layout. But these three rules are really the critical ones.
We're taking our three main content modules (.welcome, .blog,
and .gallery), and setting them to roughly half (49.375%) the
width of the entire page. Then, we're floating the .welcome and
.gallery modules off to the right, and the blog to the left. The
result? A design that's perfectly primed for reading on larger
displays (FIG 4.22). Our over-long line lengths have been reined
in, and the blog—the key piece of content—has been brought
higher on the page, making it considerably more accessible.

In other words, our responsive design is finished.

A NOTE ABOUT COMPATIBILITY

After covering media queries for not a few pages, I suppose we
should briefly quash a few dreams—I mean, um, we should
probably talk about browser support.

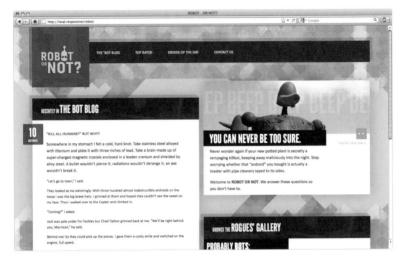

FIG 4.22: We've revisited our design, considering how widescreen readers might best experience it—and all with a quick media query.

The good news? Media queries enjoy remarkably broad support in modern desktop browsers. Opera has supported media queries since version 9.5, Firefox 3.5 and above supports them, as do WebKit-based desktop browsers like Safari 3+ and Chrome. Even Internet Explorer 9 (http://bkaprt.com/rwd2/34/) supports media queries (http://bkaprt.com/rwd2/35/)! Somebody pinch me.

And moving beyond the desktop, things are also looking good for media queries. WebKit-based mobile browsers, such as Mobile Safari, HP's webOS, and Android's browser all support media queries. And as reported by Peter-Paul Koch (http://bkaprt.com/rwd2/36/), Opera Mobile and Opera Mini are on the @media bandwagon, as are Mozilla's forays into mobile browsing. And with Windows Phone due to get IE9 in 2011 (http://bkaprt.com/rwd2/37/), we're facing a browser landscape that enjoys widespread support for media queries, which is incredibly exciting.

But sadly, "widespread" doesn't mean "universal." In desktop-based browsers older than the version numbers listed above, we're out of luck. And no, Internet Explorer doesn't provide native media query support in versions 8 and below. And while nearly all modern small-screen devices offer decent support, some legacy browsers don't understand media queries (http://bkaprt.com/rwd2/38/).

So things are far from perfect. But that doesn't mean that responsive layouts are a pipe dream. First and foremost, there are a number of JavaScript-based solutions that patch older browsers' lack of support. Personally, I've been using a script called respond.js (http://bkaprt.com/rwd2/39/), a nimble little library developed by Scott Jehl. Respond patches support for min-width and max-width queries in older browsers. And that works perfectly for most of the queries I write these days.

In fact, by dropping the respond.js library into the head of our page, we've now got a responsive layout working beautifully in older, query-blind browsers like Internet Explorer 7 (FIG 4.23).

Now, I'm not one to rely on JavaScript, and I suggest you take the same approach. We can quote stats at each other until we're blue in the face, but there's simply no guarantee that a user will have JavaScript available in their browser. Their desktop or laptop might be locked down by draconian IT security measures. And once we start looking beyond the desktop, to mobile phones, popular proxy browsers, and other devices, JavaScript support is notoriously scant, bordering on nonexistent in many devices. Or maybe their device *supports* JavaScript, but it's on an incredibly slow or spotty network. What happens when they lose their connection while downloading our JavaScript? (http://bkaprt.com/rwd2/40/)

In the hopes of addressing those issues, we'll spend some time in Chapter 5 discussing workarounds that are less reliant on JavaScript. But ultimately, it's completely understandable if JavaScript-based patches don't appeal to you. However, that only highlights the need to build your responsive design atop a flexible foundation, ensuring your design has *some* measure of device and resolution independence.

FIG 4.23: With our JavaScript patch in place, older browsers like IE now have some semblance of support for media queries.

WHY GO FLEXIBLE?

If you'll permit me one fanboyish outburst: media queries are downright awesome. They let us conditionally serve up CSS based on the capabilities of the device rendering our sites, allowing us to more fully tailor our design to our users' reading environment.

However, *media queries alone do not a responsive design make.* A truly responsive design begins with a flexible layout, with media queries layered upon that non-fixed foundation. There are a number of arguments for this, most notably that a flexible layout provides a rich fallback for JavaScript- and @media-blind devices and browsers.

But that's not the only reason. When the software company Basecamp began experimenting with a responsive design for one of their applications, they had this to say (http://bkaprt. com/rwd2/41/):

> As it turned out, making the layout work on a variety of devices was just a matter of adding a few CSS media queries to the finished product. The key to making it easy was that the layout was already liquid, so optimizing it for small screens meant collapsing a few margins to maximize space and tweaking the sidebar layout in the cases where the screen is too narrow to show two columns.

In other words, starting from a flexible foundation means *we have less code to produce.* When working with media queries, fixed-width layouts often need to be re-coded at every resolution breakpoint, whereas a design built with percentages, not pixels, maintains its proportions from one resolution to the next. As we've seen in this chapter, we can selectively remove or change the properties at each breakpoint, optimizing our layout with a few quick edits.

What's more, a flexible layout is better prepared for devices that haven't yet launched. The tablet market first arrived with the launch of the iPad, and captured our imagination as other, smaller tablets like the Galaxy Tab and Kindle hit the market. And since then, we've seen the development of burgeoning markets for wearable, internet-connected devices (http://bkaprt. com/rwd2/42/), for web-enabled smart TVs (http://bkaprt.com/ rwd2/43/), and for other browsing contexts that, a few short years ago, would have sounded like science fiction.

But this is the challenge facing us: we simply can't keep up with the different resolutions and form factors entering the marketplace. The web is, after all, meant to be viewed everywhere. A flexible layout provides us with a foundation for the future: it allows us to step back from targeting individual resolutions, and better prepare our designs for devices that haven't even been imagined yet.

Establish constraints as needed

With that said, nobody knows your design—and its users—better than you do. If you feel that placing a max-width on an element will help it maintain its integrity, go right ahead. Here's Basecamp describing their responsive experiments again (http:// bkaprt.com/rwd2/41/):

The CSS max-width property seems almost forgotten in the web designer's toolbox since it wasn't supported by Internet Explorer 6. With that restriction lifted, it's the perfect complement to a liquid layout, letting the content re-flow naturally at a variety of widths but not expanding to the point of absurdity where extreme line lengths make reading a chore. It's a great compromise between liquid and fixed layouts.

FIG 4.24: The *Boston Globe* responsive design is completely flexible—but only up to a certain width. A flexible foundation, but with a light constraint. Nice.

Similar discussions have popped up on most responsive design projects I've worked on. For example, on *The Boston Globe's* responsive site (http://bostonglobe.com/) the design has a fixed `max-width` of `1200px`, but is completely flexible below that point (**FIG 4.24**). So why not make it completely fluid? Well, we spent a lot of time considering how the page would look when it passed certain breakpoints. And the media queries we put in place reflected that design thinking, ensuring the site would be as pleasing to read on the latest build of Chrome as on an Android phone or a Kindle's browser. But ultimately, we decided we didn't have the audience to justify the time and resources required to make a compelling widescreen design. So we decided to introduce the `max-width` constraint.

What's that? You'd like to see a few live examples of the marriage of `max-width` and media queries? Well, I guess I'd have to mention Dan Cederholm's site (http://simplebits.com/), Frank Chimero's lovely design (http://frankchimero.com/), and design agency Happy Cog's official blog (http://cognition.happycog .com/) (**FIGS 4.25, 4.26** and **4.27**). Each are beautiful examples of this hybrid approach to flexible layouts, starting with a fluid grid that's eventually constrained by a pixel-based `max-width`.

Some designers prefer this method, maintaining that long line lengths are too unruly and uncomfortable to read. And frankly, they're right—but the max-width property is only one solution to that problem. Take designer and illustrator Jon Hicks' site (**FIG 4.28**), one of the first responsive redesigns launched in 2010 (http://bkaprt.com/rwd2/44/).

FIG 4.25: Dan Cederholm, the web designer's web designer, decided to set a max-width of 900 pixels on his newly responsive redesign. And you know what? It *works*.

FIG 4.26: Frank Chimero's winningly responsive design has a complex, fluid grid, but he's capped it at a rather stately 85rem.

FIG 4.27: Those talented scamps at Happy Cog recently launched a responsive blog design, deciding a max-width of 820 pixels was appropriate. The result? It's purty.

FIG 4.28: Jon Hicks' responsive site is completely flexible, and a stunner at any resolution.

FIG 4.29: Instead of relying on max-width, Jon opted to adjust his typography in certain resolution ranges, which makes for a pleasing measure *and* line length no matter how his blog is read.

I've been wanting a fluid layout on t a brief redesign back in 2005 where months, but it was soon switched ba right.

Last year, I discovered CSS media qu internal pages of the Opera Browser It was half-assed and was removed,

It took Ethan Marcotte's excellent ar Responsive Web Design to motivat as know HOW to do it properly. I dc exciting and inspirational for a long working on the basic skeleton of the resolution dependant layouts in pla design (making a few changes long t

I've been wanting a fluid layout brief redesign back in 2005 whe but it was soon switched back to

Last year, I discovered CSS medi internal pages of the Opera Brov It was half-assed and was remov

It took Ethan Marcotte's excellen Responsive Web Design to mo know HOW to do it properly. I d exciting and inspirational for a l working on the basic skeleton of resolution dependant layouts in

FIG 4.30: Jon Hicks' responsive "Shelf" theme for WordPress and Tumblr (http://bkaprt.com/ rwd2/45/) has a beautifully flexible layout, but contains fixed-width containers for different kinds of entries. (Love that horizontal scrolling!)

While there isn't a `max-width` constraining his design, Jon has instead tweaked the typography at different resolution ranges, finely tuning the leading and `font-size` to ensure his words are still a pleasure to read—all without placing any constraints on his design (**FIG. 4.29**). In other words, the flexibility of a design doesn't have to be a liability. Instead, it can be another opportunity to practice our craft, to better communicate with a certain class of users, or to solve another set of problems affecting a particular type of device.

But still, these are the kinds of decisions we constantly make as designers, choosing between flexibility and control. What responsive design shows us, however, is that it doesn't need to a binary proposition; we can have designs founded upon a flexible layout, while still including fixed-width elements (**FIG 4.30**). So when and if my client decides their audience would benefit from a widescreen layout, they could easily lift the current `max-width` constraint, create another media query, and design a compelling experience.

In other words, our designs can respond to our users' needs as quickly as we need them to.

5 BECOMING RESPONSIVE

" *The Way is shaped by use,*
But then the shape is lost.
Do not hold fast to shapes
But let sensation flow into the world
As a river courses down to the sea."
— DAO DE JING, SECTION 32, "SHAPES"

BY NOW, you have all the tools you need to start building responsive layouts. You've mastered the proportional thinking behind the flexible grid, investigated a few strategies for incorporating fixed-width media into your design, and explored how media queries can bring our designs beyond the desktop.

But up until this point, we've been looking at responsive design in a vacuum. In this chapter, let's look at some different ways to begin incorporating it into our work, as well as a few paths to improve on some of the techniques we've already discussed.

A MATTER OF CONTEXT

As you begin experimenting, you'll find that responsive designs, when properly built, can provide your visitors with a high level of continuity between different contexts. That's because, at its most basic level, responsive design is about serving one HTML document to countless browsers and devices, using flexible layouts and media queries to ensure that design is as portable and accessible as possible.

However, certain web designers argue against this approach, suggesting that different devices should always be served different markup. In a rather lengthy blog post, mobile developer James Pearce questions the merits of responsive design (http://bkaprt.com/rwd2/46/):

> The fact that the user has a small screen in their hand is one thing—the fact that it is in their hand at all is another. The fact that the user may be walking, driving, or lounging is yet another. In fact, it's quite likely that they really deserve different content and services altogether—or, at least, a differently prioritized version of the default desktop experience.

Jeff Croft (http://bkaprt.com/rwd2/47/) puts it much more succinctly:

> By and large, mobile users want different things from your product than desktop users do. If you're a restaurant, desktop users may want photos of your place, a complete menu, and some information about your history. But mobile users probably just want your address and operating hours.

There are two prongs to this argument: first, that the device implies a *context,* telling us whether the user is stationary or mobile. From that context, we can create a class of users, and infer a set of goals. In other words, mobile users will want quicker access to different tasks than they would if they were on a desktop or laptop, where both time and bandwidth are on their side.

Second, if the user's priorities and goals do indeed differ from one context to the next, then serving one HTML document to everyone won't cut it. Take Jeff's example: if the restaurant site features photos prominently at the top of every page, then chances are good that they're near the top of the HTML. Which means that a mobile visitor, when presented with the same markup in a more linear fashion, will have to do a considerable amount of scrolling just to find the hours of operation they wanted.

For what it's worth, I agree with these arguments—but up to a point. It's absolutely fair to assume a user's context from their device, but it's just that: an assumption. For example, much of my "mobile" browsing happens on the couch in my living room, flipping idly through sites on my wireless network. Now, this isn't just another of my "Ethan doesn't have a life" jokes: research has shown that a significant percentage of people use "the mobile web" from the comfort of their home (http://bkaprt. com/rwd2/48/, http://bkaprt.com/rwd2/49/). And it's not just the "mobile context" that's fuzzy, either: what does a "desktop" user look like, anyway? Sure, they might be seated at a desk, with a high-speed connection available to them—or they might be tethered to a phone, or connected to a spotty hotel network. "Mobile" and "desktop" are useful shorthand terms, but they're just that—shorthand terms that can, if we're not careful, mask a lot of complexity.

Now, that's not to say that the context question isn't valuable, or that we shouldn't be thinking about these difficult questions. But we can't simply infer a user's context from a class of devices—in many cases, the implementation of these separate, "context-aware" sites can be lacking (**FIG 5.1**). What's more, we can't neatly silo our audiences into device-specific groups: a visitor to our sites may return at multiple points throughout her day, using whatever screen happens to be nearest (http://bkaprt. com/rwd2/50/). In other words, relying upon all-too-convenient terms like "mobile" and "desktop" is no substitute for conducting the proper research into how *your* audience accesses *your* site: not only the devices and browsers they use, but how, where, and why they use them.

FIG 5.1: When viewed on an iPad, YouTube and Twitter currently default to feature-light "mobile" sites. Great design, but is it the right context?

But most importantly, responsive web design isn't intended to serve as a replacement for mobile web sites. Responsive design is, I believe, one part design philosophy, one part front-end development strategy. And as a development strategy, it's meant to be evaluated to see if it meets the needs of the project you're working on. Perhaps there's a compelling reason to keep your site's desktop and mobile experiences separate, or perhaps your content would be better served by a responsive approach. Only you and your users know for certain.

So while I agree with mobile web designers who say that certain users of certain sites deserve different content, I think the reverse is also true: many sites can *benefit* from serving one document up to multiple contexts or devices. And those are the perfect candidates for a responsive approach.

So how do you know if responsive design is right for you?

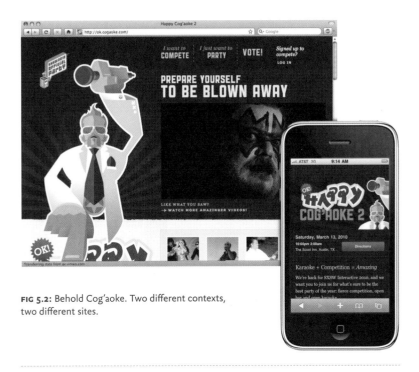

FIG 5.2: Behold Cog'aoke. Two different contexts, two different sites.

Know thy users' goals

In early 2010 I worked on a site called Cog'aoke (**FIG 5.2**), designed to promote a karaoke event hosted by my then-employer. Its main purpose was to provide visitors with information about the party, its sponsors, and its venue. But there was an application component as well: visitors could sign up to perform at the event, browse through the available catalog of songs, and vote for other prospective performers.

We also decided that the site needed a mobile-friendly component. But we envisioned something completely different from the desktop-specific site. We realized people stumbling to our event would need quick and ready access to the directions. Furthermore, we were going to have a live voting event at the show, and invite the audience to rate their favorite performer at a certain time—all through our site, accessed via their mobile phone.

As we were planning the site, it helped us to think of the desktop site as the "pre-game" experience. The mobile site, on the other hand, was really intended for the night of the event, for attendees who were physically present. So the goals of the two different contexts couldn't have been more distinct.

With that in mind, it definitely would have been *possible* for us to include all the markup for each context on every page of the site. If we'd taken that route, every page would have had the regular "desktop" content marked up in its HTML, as well as the map, directions, and voting information for the mobile site. And with those two modes baked into every HTML page, we could have used some combination of media queries and `display: none` to deliver the two sites to the right devices.

But that wouldn't have been the right approach. We realized it would have been irresponsible of us to ask our visitors to download all that extraneous HTML, marking up content that they'd never see, much less benefit from. And I don't say that just out of concern for mobile visitors: regardless of whether our visitors were on a phone- or a desktop-based browser, we would have been penalizing them with extra markup.

MEET "MOBILE FIRST"

When you have a free moment (and a stiff drink in hand), I recommend browsing through Merlin Mann's "Noise to Noise Ratio" Flickr set (http://bkaprt.com/rwd2/51/). These screen grabs showcase some of the most content-saturated pages on the web; the pages are drowning in a sea of cruft. And the actual article, both paragraphs of it, is nigh unfindable.

While the sites in Merlin's gallery might be new to you, I wager the problems they demonstrate are pretty familiar. What's more, I think this trend informs some of our preconceptions about designing for "mobile" users: namely, we assume mobile users need less content in part because desktop users can tolerate more. After all, screens are larger, users are often more stationary, and can generally better focus on searching for the content they want.

But just because desktop users *can* sift through more content, does that mean they need to? In other words, why is easy access to key tasks only the domain of mobile users? Why can't *all* users of our sites enjoy the same level of focused, curated content? Toward the end of 2009, designer Luke Wroblewski fired off a little challenge to our industry, suggesting a website's mobile experience shouldn't be an afterthought (http://bkaprt.com/ rwd2/52/). Citing the explosive growth of mobile web traffic, as well as the exciting new technical capabilities of modern phones, Luke suggested that instead today's web professionals should begin designing for *mobile first*.

"Mobile first" is a wonderful design philosophy. What's more, I've found it absolutely invaluable for the responsive design projects I've worked on. As more browsers and devices begin accessing our designs, and as our clients become interested in designing beyond the desktop, it's a perfect opportunity to take a hard look at how we design for the web: our processes and vocabulary, as well as the questions we ask and the solutions we apply.

TOWARD A RESPONSIVE WORKFLOW

Of course, these are early days yet. Many designers, studios, and companies are still learning about responsive design. As a result, we don't have many "best practices" to share within our community. That'll change over time, as we start thinking more responsively in our work. So in the meantime, I thought I'd share some of my experiences working with a more responsive workflow. Perhaps they'll be helpful to you, and (more likely) you'll find a way to improve upon them.

As I first began writing this, I was working on the redesign of a large, content-rich site. Over the course of a given day, a reader might access the site from home in the morning over coffee, read an article or two during their morning train commute, and possibly check in a few more times during the day.

Given the diversity of their readership, the client decided that a responsive approach would be the most appropriate one for their audience. So during the planning phases, the design team has taken a hard look at every proposed piece of content for the site, and asked one question: *How does this content or feature benefit our mobile users?*

Okay, maybe I should've made that sound a bit more exciting—I never was especially good at marketing. But it's a question we've derived from the "mobile first" approach, and one we've found incredibly useful as the site's designed. Here's Luke's rationale for the value of this thinking in site planning (http:// bkaprt.com/rwd2/53/):

> *If you design mobile first, you create agreement on what matters most. You can then apply the same rationale to the desktop/ laptop version of the web site. We agreed that this was the most important set of features and content for our customers and business—why should that change with more screen space?*

It's all too easy to fill a desktop browser window with social media toolbars, links to related articles, battalions of RSS links, and tag clouds galore. (This process is called "adding value," I believe.) But when we're forced to work with a screen that's 80% smaller than our usual canvas, nonessential content and cruft quickly fall away, allowing us to focus on the truly critical aspects of our designs.

In other words, designing for mobile devices first can enrich the experience for all users, by providing the element often missing from modern web design: focus. That's not to say that our client's pages are light on content, or lacking in features. But by framing our design process with that simple question, we've gained a handy acid test to apply when considering each proposed element, each new piece of functionality.

Iterative, collaborative design

Now, most design projects follow some version of the "waterfall" project management workflow, dividing the work into distinct, task-based phases. The specifics might change from one studio to the next, but there are usually four segments: a planning phase, a design phase, a development phase, and then, finally, delivery of the finished site. In each phase, documents or files are created—for example, a site map and wireframes during the planning phase—which the client approves before the next phase of work begins.

Again, the way you manage your projects might differ slightly. But for the design phase, the design team often mocks up a number of pages in a graphics editor like Photoshop, Fireworks, or the like. And once those mockups are finished and approved, they're handed off to the development team, ready to be produced into static HTML templates.

But for a responsive site, that process can quickly become a bit unwieldy. Let's pretend for a moment you're redesigning a site with only one page, so you knock out a mockup in your favorite design application. But how do you communicate to your client how that page will appear on a phone? Or an iPad? Or a widescreen display? If you've the time, budget, and resources, it might be feasible for you to design each of those alternate views, presenting those comps to the client, gathering feedback, and then revising each as needed. But if you're designing fifteen pages, or fifty, then it can quickly become impractical to produce every one of those mockups and their alternate views.

Recently, the responsive projects I've worked on have had a lot of success combining design and development into one hybrid phase, bringing the two teams into one highly collaborative group. I refer to this new, Voltron-esque phase as "designopment." (No, not really.)

Our reviews begin with the design team presenting a page mockup to the entire group. This will typically be a desktop-centric design (**FIG 5.3**), although occasionally we might start with a more mobile-focused layout. The goal is to get a starting point in front of the entire group, to kick off a discussion about how this design will need to accommodate different resolution ranges and input types. Questions tend to fly back and forth pretty rapidly: "How do you envision this slideshow working on a touch device?" "Is this module always going to be collapsed by default, or will widescreen users need to see more information?" "How will this element look (and function) if JavaScript isn't available?"

The open questions are a really great forum for the team to share ideas, to discuss how the design is intended to function on different displays, and to review any particularly complex

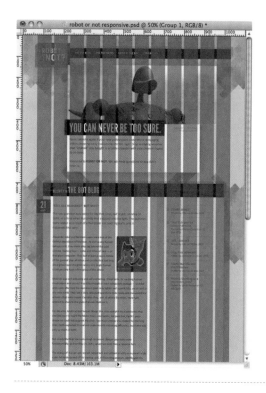

FIG 5.3: We'll begin by reviewing a finished page comp, asking questions about how it should respond to different devices and browsers.

pieces of interaction. If any design feedback needs action, then the design gets revised. But if the group feels comfortable, or if the revisions are sufficiently minor, then the development team inherits the comps for some prototyping.

"Prototyping before the designs are final, you say?" Absolutely, I say. Our goal is to get beyond the pixel limitations of Photoshop, and begin building a design that can flex and grow inside a changing browser window, that can scale to different devices. So the development team quickly begins producing a responsive design: converting the fixed grid into a fluid one, discussing ways to flexibly handle different types of media, and then finally applying the media queries that adapt our design to different resolution ranges.

Once our media queries are in place, we're constantly resizing our browser window to approximate how the designs will

FIG 5.4: As we've discussed, resizing your browser window is a great way to quickly test your design. But it's only the first step.

Outline ▾ · 🔲 Resize ▾ · 🔧 Tools ▾ · 📄 View Source ▾ · 🗋

Display Window Size
Display Window Size In Title

Resize Window...

1024x768
800x600
640x480
iPhone (portrait)
iPhone (landscape)
iPad (portrait)
iPad (landscape)

Edit Resize Dimensions...

Zoom ▸

FIG 5.5: The "Resize" menu in the Web Developer Toolbar, with a few frequently used viewport sizes.

hold up at different resolution ranges (FIG 5.4). Browser resizing extensions, such as the one included in the Web Developer Toolbar for Firefox and Chrome (http://bkaprt.com/rwd2/54/), can be a huge help here; you can even store common screen resolutions in the extension for quick access later on (FIG 5.5). But if browser extensions and whatnot aren't your thing, you might try Dave Rupert's fitWeird bookmarklet (http://bkaprt. com/rwd2/55/) or Jordan Moore's "Responsive Roulette" viewer (http://bkaprt.com/rwd2/56/), which, in addition to being well-made tools, beautifully reinforce that your responsive design could be encountered on screens of any size.

But as we discussed in the last chapter, resizing your browser window is really an intermediary step. If you want to test how your page is going to perform on a given device, there's no substitute for viewing it on the actual device. (If you're interested in setting up a mobile testing suite, I highly recommend Peter-Paul Koch's *A List Apart* article on the "Smartphone Browser Landscape" (http://bkaprt.com/rwd2/57/), or Brad Frost's tips on smartly investing in mobile devices (http://bkaprt.com/rwd2/58/). And if you're not interested in buying a small army of phones and tablets and whatnot, why not use http://opendevicelab.com/ to see if there's an open device lab near you?)

During this development process, a prototype begins to take shape. It's based on the initial mockup supplied by the design team, of course, but as the development team codes they begin making recommendations about how the design should respond to different devices. In other words, during this collaboration the developers act as designers, too; they're just designing in a different medium. They're making design recommendations within the browser, rather than in Photoshop—recommendations that will be shared, tested, and vetted by the entire team.

Now, the prototype doesn't have to be completely tested or production-ready. Because once that template's somewhat finished, we start another design review—but this time, the design and development teams are reviewing code, not comps.

The interactive design review

To prepare for this meeting, we'll load up the prototype page on several phones, tablets, laptops, and other devices (FIG 5.6). When the meeting begins, the development team will introduce the page to the group, and then let everyone have at it. Because during the rest of the review, the entire group experiments with the design: on laptops and desktops, on phones and tablets. We'll resize our browser windows, swipe through photo galleries, and test how usable forms are on both keyboards and touch screens.

But while everyone's experimenting with the prototype, we try to keep a steady flow of conversation going. I've found it helps if the development team has a list of questions that came up as they were building the responsive design. Perhaps they noticed that a crucial link is a little too difficult to hit on a touch screen, or a maybe an animation is moving a little too slowly on a particular desktop browser. Calling out areas of interest or

FIG 5.6: The devices used in the jQuery Mobile testing suite. (Courtesy Filament Group, Inc., http://bkaprt.com/rwd2/59/.)

potential sticking points, and then asking for feedback, is a great way to get people talking about how well the design performs, and how it generally feels.

Because ultimately, the purpose of these reviews is to help vet the "live" design. After all, the initial mockup was used as a blueprint, providing layout rules, a typographic guide, and a pattern library; from there, the development team was responsible for adapting the design into its more responsive incarnation. In other words, we're testing the design recommendations made by the development team, and discussing whether further refinement is needed. That refinement could either be a revised mockup, or some tweaks in the template. And once the meeting is finished, the two halves of the group decamp with their respective feedback, and the process repeats itself. Review, design, build, and repeat.

Here's a hypothetical example of how this back-and-forth works. Let's say the design team has mocked up a global navigation module, which includes a couple of key links and a search field. And with that comp in hand, the development team has dutifully built the navigation into the template (**FIG. 5.7**).

The design's fairly straightforward, calling for two links displayed inline, with the search field to their right. And in making the design responsive, the development team settles on a fairly modest solution for smaller displays, choosing to give the search bar the full width of the page, and centering the two links beneath it (**FIG. 5.8**).

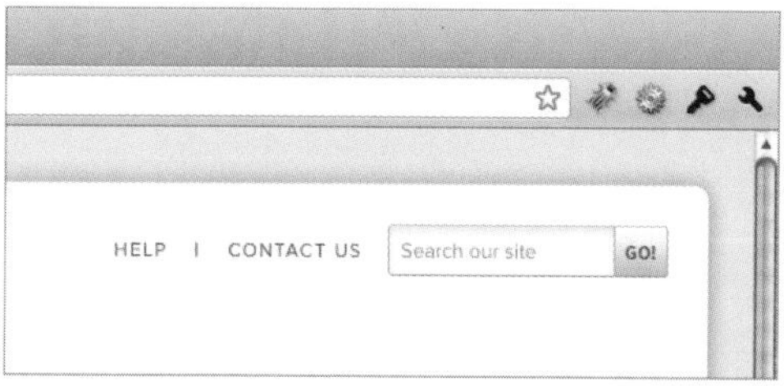

FIG 5.7: The "desktop" view of the newly designed global navigation bar.

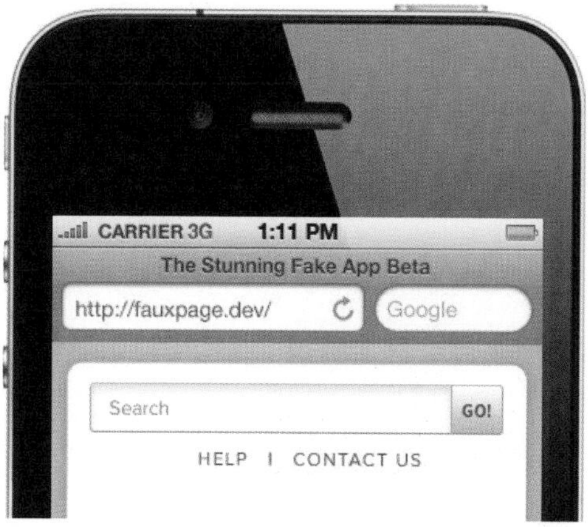

FIG 5.8: At smaller resolution breakpoints, the links were initially placed beneath the search bar.

During the design review, a few design team members ask about the smaller version of the global navigation, as something about the elements' placement feels a bit off to them. The search bar is considerably more prominent, sure, but some of the folks feel that maybe it's *too* prominent, crowding out the links beneath it. And in fact, once they started interacting with the design on touch-enabled phones, they realize it's a little too easy to tap into the search field when trying to activate a link.

So the coded version of the navigation isn't quite working. And after discussing it for a bit, the design team comes up with an alternate solution (**FIG 5.9**). Instead of displaying the search bar at smaller resolutions, they decide to collapse it by default, making it appear as though it was just another link in the menu.

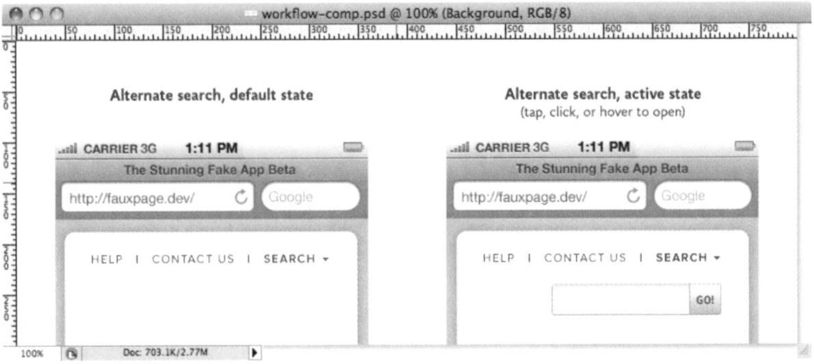

FIG 5.9: After discussing the problems at hand, the design team comes up with an alternate design for our problematic little navigation bar.

FIG 5.10: Our finished navigation bar, iteratively built by designers and developers.

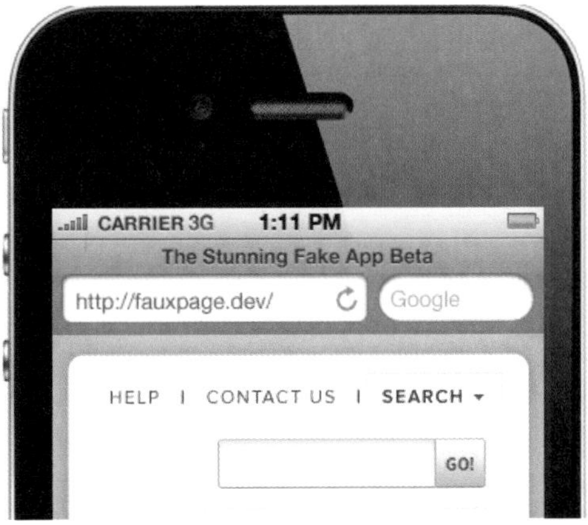

But when that label is tapped or clicked on, the search bar appears as a drop-down beneath the rest of the menu (FIG 5.10).

That's just one brief example of how this more collaborative approach can work. The key is to make this design/development cycle as iterative as it needs to be, with both groups constantly refining their work, and then sharing it with the group for review. For the project I'm working on, we've been meeting weekly for our interactive design reviews, but we're constantly sharing sketches—whether in design or in code—via email throughout the week.

Ultimately, the goal is to close the gap between the traditional "design" and "development" cycles, and let the two groups collaborate more closely to produce a finished, responsive design. This more agile approach has allowed the groups I've worked on to use applications like Photoshop for design direction and guidance, but then quickly move into our real canvas: the browser.

BEING RESPONSIVE, RESPONSIBLY

During our design/development cycle, the pages are constantly being refined as we build them, with the goal of finishing the phase with production-ready templates. And as we code our responsive design, we've found the philosophy of "mobile first" to be incredibly important.

Throughout the book, we've been using the Robot or Not site to demonstrate how a fluid grid, flexible images, and media queries work together to provide a more responsive approach to design. We began by taking our rigid mockup, designed in Photoshop, and converting it into a fluid grid. As we saw in Chapter 4, that caused no end of problems when we started resizing our browser window; our initial design wasn't intended to scale beyond its original context. So we introduced media queries to address those issues, and to provide alternate small- and widescreen layouts. And finally, for browsers lacking native support for media queries, we included the `respond.js` library to provide access to our alternate designs.

However, this approach raises another very real problem: what if an `@media`-blind browser doesn't have access to JavaScript? In that case, they'd be forced to render our full, desktop-centric design, regardless of whether that's appropriate for their device. And for many mobile devices, that's exactly what they'd see: a design intended for a much wider screen, shoehorned into a tiny space (**FIG 5.11**).

And there's another problem with the way we've built the site. Here's a brief snippet from the CSS:

FIG 5.11: No media queries? No JavaScript? No good: our flexible, desktop-friendly layout tries to cram into a small space.

```
.blog {
  background: #F8F5F2 url("img/blog-bg.png") repeat-y;
}

@media screen and (max-width: 768px) {
  .blog {
    background: #F8F5F2 url("img/noise.gif");
  }
}
```

First, we're setting a background image on the `.blog` element. (Specifically, the two-toned `blog-bg.png` graphic we used in Chapter 2 to create the illusion of two columns.) Then for smaller displays, those narrower than `768px` wide, we're instead placing a simple tiled GIF on the blog element, since we've linearized the display of those narrower pages.

The problem with this approach is that some browsers will actually download *both* graphics, even if only one is ultimately applied to the page (see developer Tim Kadlec's tests for more info: `http://bkaprt.com/rwd2/60/`). While smaller screens don't always equate to lower bandwidth, we might be punishing users on smaller screens with the download of a much heavier image than they'll ever see.

Thankfully, these aren't problems with responsive design in and of itself—we just need to rethink the way we've implemented it.

"Mobile first" meets media queries

Speaking broadly, responsive design is about starting from a *reference resolution,* and using media queries to adapt it to other contexts. A more responsible approach to responsive design would mean building our stylesheet with "mobile first" in mind, rather than defaulting to a desktop layout. So we'd begin by defining a layout appropriate to smaller screens, and then use media queries to progressively enhance our design as the resolution increases.

In fact, we took this approach on the responsive site for *The Boston Globe* (`http://www.bostonglobe.com/`). By default, the content is arranged in a very linear manner, one friendly to mobile devices and narrow browser windows (**FIG 5.12**). But as the viewport widens, the grid becomes more complex (**FIG 5.13**). And at the highest end of the spectrum, the "full" design finally reveals itself: the layout becomes even more complex, making for a truly widescreen display (**FIG 5.14**).

The design is still responsive, using all of the techniques we've discussed thus far in this book: the layout is based on

FIG 5.12: The small-screen-friendly foundation of BostonGlobe.com: a vertically-sorted list of tasks and content, with very little layout to speak of.

a fluid grid, and the images still work well within that flexible context. But in contrast to the Robot or Not site, we're applying `min-width` media queries to scale our design *up* through the resolution spectrum. The basic structure of the stylesheet looks something like this:

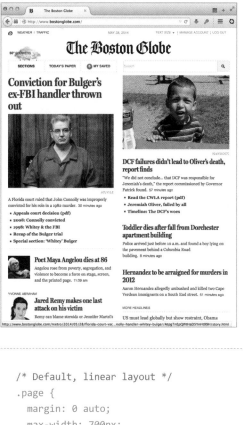

FIG 5.13: As the viewport gets a little wider, the bostonglobe.com layout gets slightly more complex, using `min-width` queries to make better use of the available space.

```
/* Default, linear layout */
.page {
  margin: 0 auto;
  max-width: 700px;
      background: #fff;
  position: relative;
}

/* Small screen! */
@media screen and (min-width: 480px) { … }
@media screen and (min-width: 620px) { … }
@media screen and (min-width: 810px) { … }
@media screen and (min-width: 1400px) { … }
```

The bulk of the stylesheet contains little else but color- and type-related rules, providing a basic (but hopefully still attractive)

FIG 5.14: At wider screens, another set of min-width queries reshapes the layout again, converting bostonglobe.com to a widescreen-friendly layout. By beginning with a small-screen-ready layout, each breakpoint builds on the one preceding it, leaving us with an accessible *and* responsive design.

design to all users. In other words: outside of the media queries, the stylesheet begins with a linear, small-screen-friendly design by *default,* one that doesn't have much of a layout to speak of. But then, breakpoints are set in a series of min-width media queries, for minimum viewport widths of 480px, 620px, 810px, and 1400px. And as the viewport scales up beyond those thresholds, the appropriate layout rules are applied. The benefit to this approach? If a browser without media query support accesses the Globe, they're given an attractive, single-column layout if our JavaScript patch isn't available to them (**FIG 5.15**).

What if we wanted to take this approach with our little Robot site? Converting the entire design to small-screen-friendly breakpoints is beyond the scope of this short book, but let's walk through a simple layout. Here's the CSS we're currently using to control the two-column layout for our blog:

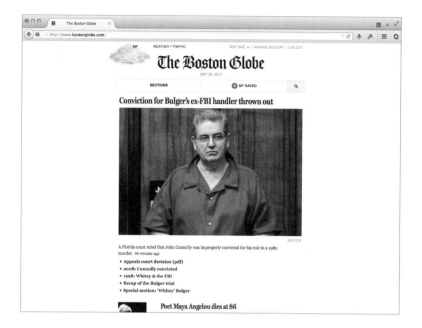

FIG 5.15: No media queries? No JavaScript? No problem: designing for the small screen first means *every* browser is left with an accessible design, regardless of the size of its screen.

```css
.blog .main {
  float: left;
  width: 62.8888889%;      /* 566px / 900px */
}
.blog .other {
  float: right;
  width: 36.7777778%;      /* 331px / 900px */
}
@media screen and (max-width: 768px) {
  .blog .main,
  .blog .other {
    float: none;
    width: auto;
  }
}
```

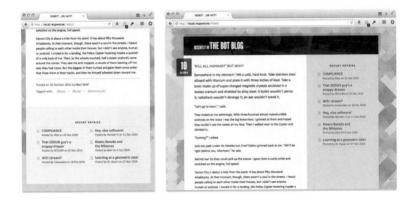

FIG 5.16: Our blog layout now *defaults* to a linear, small-screen-friendly design, but then moves to a two-column layout only when seen above a certain viewport width. The result is the same, but the code is much more accessible.

In other words, our `.main` and `.other` elements—the blog entry, and the list of recent entries that follows it—are floated columns by default, unless the viewport is narrower than 768px. (@media screen and (max-width: 768px) { … }.) If it falls below that threshold, we disable our floats, set the `width` of the two elements back to `auto`, and allow them to stack vertically on smaller screens. (**FIG. 5.16**)

But what if we wanted to adopt a more "mobile first" approach to this same layout? Thankfully, it's easily done:

```
@media screen and (min-width: 768px) {
  .blog .main {
    float: left;
    width: 62.8888889%;    /* 566px / 900px */
  }
  .blog .other {
    float: right;
    width: 36.7777778%;    /* 331px / 900px */
  }
}
```

All we've done is take the floats and widths for our two-column layout, and moved them into a `min-width` media query—not a `max-width` query, as we did before. The result is that the two-column layout will apply *only* if the screen is at least 768px wide. In other words, we're not using our media query to *override* rules from wider breakpoints; we're using it to layer complexity onto our design as viewports gradually widen. While the two approaches are visually similar, this "mobile first" approach to building responsive templates ensures greater accessibility to our content, but doesn't make any assumptions about the capabilities of the device or browser rendering our design. And after adopting it for my client projects, I've found it's the best, most bulletproof way to implement your responsive designs.

REVISITING PROGRESSIVE ENHANCEMENT

A more thorough implementation of this approach would be the responsive redesign of *The Guardian* (http://www.theguardian.com/), which is, at the time of this book's writing, in a public beta (**FIG. 5.17**). (If you're on a non-mobile device, select the "Beta" link from the site's header to see the new responsive beta.) In a conference presentation (http://bkaprt.com/rwd2/61/), *The Guardian's* Matt Andrews discussed the various ways in which responsive design changed the way their team collaborated. And there were a number of changes—from design to development, from project planning to internal communication. But for them, one of the most critical ideas was this:

> *The first step in rethinking the web for the future is accepting that making things look exactly the same across all browsers is an idea best left to the past.*

The language is different, of course, but it overlaps beautifully with Nick Finck and Steven Champeon's original definition of "progressive enhancement" (http://bkaprt.com/rwd2/62/):

> *Rather than hoping for graceful degradation, progressive enhancement builds documents for the least capable or differently capable devices first, then moves on to enhance*

FIG 5.17: Regardless of how wide or small your screen might be, or how modern or ancient your browser happens to be, *The Guardian*'s new responsive site is at once accessible and beautiful.

> those documents with separate logic for presentation, in ways
> that don't place an undue burden on baseline devices but which
> allow a richer experience for those users with modern graphical
> browser software.

Since Nick and Steven coined the term in 2003, progressive enhancement has been the hallmark of the responsible approach to standards-based web design. By beginning with a foundation of semantic, well-structured markup, styling with a layer of CSS, and adding DOM scripting via JavaScript as needed, we can create compelling experiences in capable browsers, while ensuring universal access to the content beneath the design.

In fact, progressive enhancement has been the cornerstone for most modern responsive designs. Take the BBC News website, for example: they've been experimenting with responsive

FIG 5.18: The new responsive BBC News site isn't just accessible to differently sized screens, but to high- and low-end devices and browsers alike.

design in public at http://m.bbc.com/news/, only allowing "mobile" devices to access the responsive site (FIG 5.18). In time, that responsive prototype will become the default experience for *all* their visitors—mobile, tablet, desktop, and whatever comes next. (In fact, by the time you read this, it might be the default experience already. Books are weird that way.)

The BBC News team is designing responsively on a massive scale, planning for a site that will work on the latest iOS and Android devices—as well as less capable smartphones in developing markets. And the key of their strategy is progressive enhancement: of letting even the lowest-end devices access the new responsive site, but conditionally enhancing up to an enriched experience. In 2012, they took to their development blog (http://bkaprt.com/rwd2/63/) to describe how they responsively design for a complex, sprawling device landscape:

*We have ~80 **significant** browsers / operating system combinations regularly using our application across the globe and a long tail of hundreds more.... We make this manageable in the same [way] you and everyone else in the industry does it: by having a lowest common denominator and developing towards that. So we've taken the decision to split the entire browser market into two, which we are currently calling "feature browsers" and "smart browsers".*

...

*The first tier of support we call **the core experience**. This works on everything.... As the application loads we earmark incapable browsers with [some inline code] and exclude the bulk of the Javascript powered UI from them, leaving them with clean, concise, core experience.*

In other words, the BBC News team isn't designing for specific platforms, or even focusing on device classes. Instead, they're designing for *experience tiers:* a basic design served to every device; and a more enhanced version, conditionally served to more capable browsers. The result is a responsive design that loads quickly in every HTML-capable device, but then upgrades to a more robust interface—but only if the browser is deemed capable of handling the more enhanced experience (**FIG 5.19**). And this progressive enhancement-driven approach has been the foundation of some of the largest responsive designs, including responsive sites like *The Boston Globe* and *The Guardian*.

Stephen Hay reiterated the need for progressive enhancement as well, in his fantastic essay "There is no Mobile Web" (http://bkaprt.com/rwd2/65/):

Most sites on the web are not built with specific mobile use-cases in mind. However, millions of people access these sites every day through mobile devices. They access a "normal" (whatever that means) website through their "mobile" device.

...

To be honest, I can think of a few, but not many use cases of web sites or apps which are or should be exclusively mobile.

FIG 5.19: By building with progressive enhancement, the responsive BBC News site doesn't have to focus on individual devices or platforms; instead, they can design for broad experience tiers. (Source: http://bkaprt.com/rwd2/64/)

It seems like the Mobile Web allows us to revisit all of the talk of inclusion, progressive enhancement, and accessibility from years ago.

Ever have one of those moments where someone else perfectly expresses why you believe in something? Stephen's essay manages to capture *exactly* why I'm excited about responsive web design. Rather than simply siloing our content into different, device-specific sites, we can use progressive enhancement to ensure quality access for all, with an enhanced experience for those devices that are capable of it.

Working with JavaScript

To put this to the test, let's take a look at the slideshow at the top of the Robot or Not site (FIG 5.20). Currently, the markup looks like this:

```
<div class="slides">
  <div class="figure">
    <b><img src="img/slide-robot.jpg" alt="" /></b>
    <div class="figcaption">…</div>
  </div><!-- /end .figure -->

  <ul class="carousel-nav">
    <li><a class="prev" href="#">Previous</a></li>
    <li><a class="next" href="#">Next</a></li>
  </ul>
</div><!-- /end .slides -->
```

Not too fancy. But also, not too functional: we've marked up the interface for a slideshow, but it isn't implemented yet. We've included a single slide in our template, as well as the previous/next navigation. But clicking on those links won't do a darned thing.

So, we'll need to introduce a bit of JavaScript, and bring some interactivity into our design. But first, we need slides! So, let's grab some more images, and augment our HTML a bit:

```
<div class="slides">
  <div class="figure">
    <b><img src="img/slide-robot.jpg" alt="" /></b>
    <div class="figcaption">…</div>
  </div><!-- /end .figure -->
  <div class="figure">
    <b><img src="img/slide-tin.jpg" alt="" /></b>
    <div class="figcaption">…</div>
  </div><!-- /end .figure -->
</div><!-- /end .slides -->
```

Let's drop in four more slides, using the same .figure markup pattern as before. I've also deleted the .carousel-nav element that housed our previous and next links, as we'll be adding that dynamically through our JavaScript.

So, yes, this looks a little weird right now, as our slides are currently just stacked on top of each other (FIG 5.21). To get our slideshow up and running, we'll be using a free jQuery plugin designed by Filament Group (http://bkaprt.com/rwd2/66/). It's one of the more robust slideshow scripts I've used. I like it because it works incredibly well with flexible content; if your slides have different amounts of text or images in them, this plugin handles them with ease—all without resorting to convoluted CSS foofery. (Oh, yes. I said "foofery." I'm not messing around.)

So to work the carousel script into the page, I'm going to add three new script elements to our HTML:

```
<script src="jquery.js"></script>
<script src="carousel.js"></script>
<script src="core.js"></script>
```

Since the carousel script requires jQuery to run, I've downloaded the library from http://jquery.com/ and placed it in the head of the page (jquery.js), followed by the carousel script

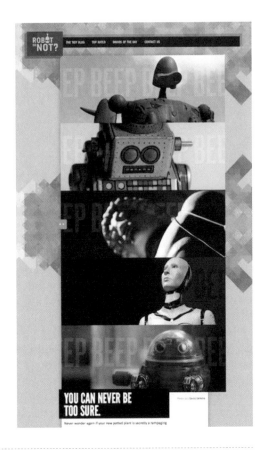

New slides: we add them. Stacked images: we hate them.

(carousel.js), and a file called core.js, which is where we'll actually write the code for our slideshow.

And actually, it's fairly easy to do. Inside of core.js, let's write the following:

```
(function( $ ) {
  $( function(){
    $( ".welcome .slides" ).carousel();
  } );
}( jQuery ));
```

FIG 5.22: The slideshow lives. It lives!

Now, if you're not completely comfortable with JavaScript, or haven't used jQuery before, that's okay. The script above is just doing two different things:

1. First, it locates the `div.slides` element inside of the `.welcome` module, using jQuery's very CSS-friendly selector syntax. (`$(".welcome .slides")`).
2. Once it has located that element, our script runs the `.carousel()` function, creating the slideshow.

And with those five short lines of JavaScript, we've got a working slideshow (**FIG 5.22**). Success!

Lazily (but intelligently) loading content

Or at least, it's a starting point. If we disable JavaScript in the browser, we're back to where we were before: with a whole mess of slides stacked on top of each other. So for any visitor to our site that doesn't have JavaScript available to them, the experience quickly becomes decidedly un-great.

So let's do something about that. In fact, let's get a bit tricky: we're going to remove all but one of the slides from the page, and put them in a separate HTML file. So now, our page's source looks considerably lighter:

```
<div class="slides">
  <div class="figure">
    <b><img src="img/slide-robot.jpg" alt="" /></b>
    <div class="figcaption">…</div>
  </div><!-- /end .figure -->
</div><!-- /end .slides -->
```

However, we've created a separate file (let's call it `slides.html`), and pasted in the markup for our four remaining slides:

```
<div class="figure">
  <b><img src="img/slide-tin.jpg" alt="" /></b>
  <div class="figcaption">…</div>
</div><!-- /end .figure -->
<div class="figure">
  <b><img src="img/slide-statue.jpg" alt="" /></b>
  <div class="figcaption">…</div>

  …
</div><!-- /end .figure -->
```

You've probably noticed that `slides.html` isn't even a valid HTML document. In fact, it's more like a markup stub, a mini-document we can use to store some HTML for later use. In fact, we'll just use jQuery to open `slides.html` and load the images into the slideshow, like so:

```
(function( $ ) {
  $( function(){
    $.get( "-/ajax/slides.html", function( data ) {
      $( ".welcome .slides" )
        .append( data )
        .carousel();
    });
  } );
}( jQuery ));
```

And that's that. The jQuery `.get()` function opens our HTML snippet (`slides.html`), and inserts its contents into our module by using `append()`. If JavaScript isn't available, or if jQuery can't

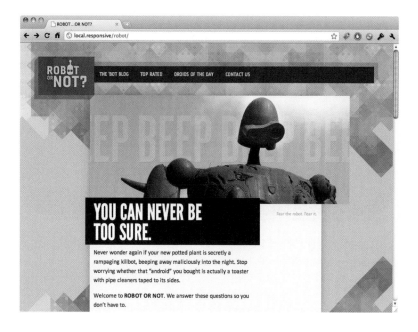

FIG 5.23: No JavaScript? No problem. Our slideshow degrades to a single image, which looks just grand.

load that file, then the user is presented with a single image at the top of the page: a perfectly acceptable fallback for our design (**FIG 5.23**).

Further improvements

We've augmented our simple slideshow script with considerably *more* code, but the end result is a much more robust and accessible experience. We're not assuming anything about the capabilities of the browser or device rendering our page: if JavaScript is available to them, then our slideshow will appear.

But there's always room for improvement—and this rough little prototype is no exception. For example, we could potentially restrict our slideshow to only appear on certain types of displays, making the script *resolution dependent*. For example, if

FIG 5.20: We've decided that our slideshow will only be available to browsers wider than 480px. Smaller screens get a single image.

we wanted to prevent it from loading at all on smaller screens, we could work a simple resolution test into our script:

```
if (document.documentElement.clientWidth >= 500) {
  $(document).ready(function() { … });
}
```

That opening if statement is the JavaScript equivalent of a min-width: 500px media query: if the screen is narrower than 500 pixels, then the enclosed JavaScript won't fire (FIG 5.24). And while we're being bandwidth-conscientious, I'd probably use the new picture element—with support patched in via Filament Group's picturefill.js library (http://bkaprt.com/rwd2/67/)—which would allow us to serve lighter, more bandwidth-friendly images to smaller displays, with the full-sized images served only to wider screens.

And we could refine this approach further. For example: instead of including three script elements in our HTML, we would ideally use a lightweight JavaScript loader like LabJS (http://labjs.com/) or yepnope (http://yepnopejs.com/) to dynamically load jQuery, the carousel plugin, and our own `custom.js`—perhaps including them only if the user's browser is sufficiently advanced. That would help ensure that users on less capable devices aren't saddled with the overhead of downloading all that JavaScript, especially if the carousel wouldn't work well for them.

GO FORTH AND BE RESPONSIVE

I mention these enhancements not because they're necessarily the right approach; in the age of portable 3G hotspots and wifi-enabled phones, it's dangerous to automatically equate a screen's dimensions with the bandwidth available to it. But if you need an extra level of resolution awareness in your work, these tools are available.

Still, I find it helpful to keep Luke's "mobile first" philosophy in mind when I'm faced with a particularly involved bit of functionality. If I'm disabling a tricky interface for mobile users, then why is there value in it for the rest of my audience? If that sounds like a loaded question, it's not meant to be: there aren't any easy answers here.

Because more than anything, web design is about asking the right questions. And really, that's what responsive web design is: a possible solution, a way to more fully design for the web's inherent flexibility. In the first chapter, I said that the ingredients for a responsive design were a fluid grid, flexible images, and media queries. But really, they're just the vocabulary we'll use to articulate answers to the problems our users face, a framework for ordering content in an ever-increasing number of devices and browsers.

If we're willing to research the needs of our users, and apply those ingredients carefully, then responsive web design is a powerful approach indeed.

I can't wait to see the stories you'll tell with it.

ACKNOWLEDGEMENTS

I don't have the words—or the space—to properly thank the people that have influenced my work, let alone this little book. Still, I have to try.

First and foremost, I'm impossibly grateful to A Book Apart for being interested in responsive design, and for offering me the chance to write my first solo book. Jason Santa Maria's attention to detail and quality is unparalleled. Katel LeDu kept me focused, on-track, and laughing, and always keeps a steady hand at A Book Apart's prow. Mandy Brown is an impossibly incisive editor, and I feel so lucky to have had her help and patience in shaping not just this book, but my first article on responsive design.

And of course, my heartfelt thanks to Jeffrey Zeldman: for his impassioned writing and tireless work, and for the opportunities they've afforded me over the years.

Karen McGrane, Peter-Paul Koch, Bryan and Stephanie Rieger, Jason Grigsby, and Stephen Hay have taught me much of what I know about designing for mobile, and improved my thinking about responsive design in countless subtle, significant ways. And for any design project, responsive or otherwise, Luke Wroblewski's work on "mobile first" is invaluable.

Khoi Vinh and Mark Boulton have taught our community—and me—much about the history behind our craft. What's more, a fluid grid would never have proven feasible without Richard Rutter's early research.

If I hadn't read John Allsopp's magnificent "A Dao Of Web Design" over a decade ago, my understanding of the web would be drastically different, and this book would have never happened.

David Sleight and the team at Filament Group provided indispensable feedback on an early draft of the book.

I'm impossibly grateful Anna Debenham agreed to act as tech editor for this second edition of the book. This little yellow book has been made all the stronger for her tireless efforts, brilliant ideas, and wonderful questions.

Dan Cederholm's technical edit of the first edition was thoughtful, thorough, and hilarious. Just like him.

I can't quite articulate how honored I am that Jeremy Keith agreed to write the foreword. Hell, "honored" doesn't even adequately cover it.

If I can form a decent sentence from time to time, it's because of Garret Keizer.

My family—my parents, my brothers, my sisters, and my grandmother—were there for me throughout the writing process. I love you guys.

And finally, to my wife Elizabeth. This book, and everything else, is for her.

RESOURCES

For a more complete history behind the typographic grid, I'd suggest the following:

- Wikipedia's entry on the canons of page construction: http://bkaprt.com/rwd2/68/
- *The New Typography* by Jan Tschichold (Second Edition, University of California Press, 2006): http://bkaprt.com/rwd2/69/
- *Grid Systems in Graphic Design* by Josef Müller-Brockmann (Verlag Niggli AG): http://bkaprt.com/rwd2/70/

In looking at how grids apply specifically to web design, I'd suggest:

- *Ordering Disorder: Grid Principles for Web Design* by Khoi Vinh (New Riders Press, 2010): http://bkaprt.com/rwd2/71/
- *A Practical Guide to Designing Grid Systems for the Web* by Mark Boulton (Five Simple Steps, forthcoming): http://bkaprt.com/rwd2/72/
- Mark Boulton's blog entry, "A Richer Canvas": http://bkaprt.com/rwd2/73/
- The Grid System: http://bkaprt.com/rwd2/74/
- My article for A List Apart on "Fluid Grids": http://bkaprt.com/rwd2/75/

Looking for a reference on media queries? While the following two links are somewhat tech-y, I think they're still accessible, fantastic reads:

- The W3C's media query specification: http://bkaprt.com/rwd2/76/
- Mozilla's developer reference on media queries: http://bkaprt.com/rwd2/77/

If you're working with images and other media in a flexible context, I recommend checking out:

- Filament Group's "Compressive Images" technique: http://bkaprt.com/rwd2/78/
- Richard Rutter's original image resizing experiments: http://bkaprt.com/rwd2/79/
- Filament Group's Picturefill library: http://bkaprt.com/rwd2/80/, with the related blog entry: http://bkaprt.com/rwd2/81/

For more information to help you decide when and how to adopt a responsive approach, I'd recommend:

- John Allsopp's seminal "A Dao of Web Design": http://bkaprt.com/rwd2/82/
- Luke Wroblewski's articles on "mobile first": http://bkaprt.com/rwd2/52/, with related readings available http://bkaprt.com/rwd2/83/
- Jeremy Keith's "One Web": http://bkaprt.com/rwd2/84/ and "Context": http://bkaprt.com/rwd2/85/
- Tim Kadlec's entry on "Responsive Web Design and Mobile Context": http://bkaprt.com/rwd2/86/
- Josh Clark (http://bkaprt.com/rwd2/87/) and Jason Grigsby (http://bkaprt.com/rwd2/88/) round up some great discussions to help you decide when a responsive approach is appropriate, and for which projects. (You should be reading Josh and Jason's blogs anyway.)
- My own blog entries on "With Good References" (http://bkaprt.com/rwd2/89/), "Toffee-Nosed" (http://bkaprt.com/rwd2/90/), and "Responsive design, screens, and shearing layers" (http://bkaprt.com/rwd2/91/).

REFERENCES

Shortened URLs are numbered sequentially; the related long URLs are listed below for reference.

Chapter 1

1 http://craigmod.com/journal/post_artifact/

2 https://www.flickr.com/photos/carabanderson/3033798968/

3 http://alistapart.com/article/dao

4 http://money.cnn.com/2014/02/28/technology/mobile/mobile-apps-internet/

5 https://speakerdeck.com/anna/playing-with-game-console-browsers?slide=6

6 http://vimeo.com/14899669

7 http://vimeo.com/14899445

8 http://www.smartglassinternational.com/

9 http://vimeo.com/4661618

10 https://gitlab.com/beep/rwd-samplefiles

Chapter 2

11 http://meyerweb.com/eric/tools/css/reset/

Chapter 3

12 https://www.flickr.com/photos/uberculture/1385828839/

13 http://clagnut.com/sandbox/imagetest/

14 http://www.cameronmoll.com/archives/000892.html

15 http://msdn.microsoft.com/en-us/library/ms532969.aspx

16 http://www.dillerdesign.com/experiment/DD_belatedPNG/

17 http://msdn.microsoft.com/en-us/library/ms532920%28VS.85%29.aspx

18 http://unstoppablerobotninja.com/entry/fluid-images/

19 http://www.yuiblog.com/blog/2008/12/08/imageopt-5/

20 http://alistapart.com/article/fauxcolumns

21 http://stopdesign.com/archive/2004/09/03/liquid-bleach.html

22 http://www.w3.org/TR/css3-background/#the-background-size

23 http://srobbin.com/jquery-plugins/backstretch/

24 http://www.bbc.co.uk/news/technology-11948680

25 http://scottjehl.github.io/picturefill/

Chapter 4

26 http://www.w3.org/TR/CSS2/media.html

27 http://alistapart.com/article/goingtoprint

28 http://www.w3.org/TR/CSS21/media.html#media-types

29 http://www.w3.org/TR/css3-mediaqueries/

30 http://www.w3.org/TR/css3-mediaqueries/#media1

31 https://developer.apple.com/library/safari/documentation/
appleapplications/reference/SafariHTMLRef/Articles/MetaTags.html

32 https://developer.mozilla.org/en-US/docs/Mozilla/Mobile/Viewport_meta_
tag#Viewport_basics

33 https://www.theleagueofmoveabletype.com/league-gothic

34 http://windows.microsoft.com/en-us/internet-explorer/download-ie

35 https://ie.microsoft.com/testdrive/HTML5/CSS3MediaQueries/

36 http://www.quirksmode.org/mobile/#t14

37 http://blogs.msdn.com/b/iemobile/archive/2011/02/14/ie9-coming-to-
windows-phone-in-2011.aspx

38 http://www.quirksmode.org/m/css.html#t021

39 https://github.com/scottjehl/Respond

40 https://twitter.com/jaffathecake/status/207096228339658752

41 http://signalvnoise.com/posts/2661-experimenting-with-responsive-design-
in-iterations

42 https://plus.google.com/+VladFilippov/posts/EPcJCN4VSi3

43 https://speakerdeck.com/grigs/the-immobile-web

44 http://hicksdesign.co.uk/journal/finally-a-fluid-hicksdesign

45 https://thethemefoundry.com/wordpress-themes/shelf/

Chapter 5

46 http://tripleodeon.com/2010/10/not-a-mobile-web-merely-a-320px-
wide-one/

47 http://jeffcroft.com/blog/2010/aug/06/responsive-web-design-and-
mobile-context/

48 http://thefonecast.com/Home/tabid/61/ArticleID/3602/ArtMID/538/
Default.aspx

49 http://www.lukew.com/ff/entry.asp?1263

50 http://www.comscore.com/Insights/Blog/The_Rise_of_Digital_Omnivores

51 https://www.flickr.com/photos/merlin/sets/72157622077100537/

52 http://www.lukew.com/ff/entry.asp?933

53 http://www.lukew.com/ff/entry.asp?1117

54 http://chrispederick.com/work/web-developer/

55 http://davatron5000.github.io/fitWeird/

56 http://www.jordanm.co.uk/lab/responsiveroulette

57 http://alistapart.com/article/smartphone-browser-landscape

58 http://bradfrostweb.com/blog/mobile/test-on-real-mobile-devices-without-breaking-the-bank/

59 https://www.flickr.com/photos/filamentgroup/5149016958/

60 http://timkadlec.com/2012/04/media-query-asset-downloading-results/

61 http://mattandrews.info/talks/canvasconf-2013/

62 http://www.hesketh.com/thought-leadership/our-publications/inclusive-web-design-future

63 http://responsivenews.co.uk/post/18948466399/cutting-the-mustard

64 http://mobiletestingfordummies.tumblr.com/post/20056227958/testing

65 http://www.the-haystack.com/2011/01/07/there-is-no-mobile-web/

66 https://github.com/filamentgroup/responsive-carousel

67 https://github.com/filamentgroup/picturefill

Resources

68 https://en.wikipedia.org/wiki/Canons_of_page_construction

69 http://www.worldcat.org/oclc/70399614

70 http://www.worldcat.org/oclc/781678237

71 http://www.worldcat.org/oclc/639165178

72 http://www.worldcat.org/oclc/713636248

73 http://www.markboulton.co.uk/journal/a-richer-canvas

74 http://www.thegridsystem.org/

75 http://alistapart.com/article/fluidgrids

76 http://www.w3.org/TR/css3-mediaqueries/

77 https://developer.mozilla.org/en-US/docs/Web/Guide/CSS/Media_queries

78 http://filamentgroup.com/lab/rwd_img_compression/

79 http://clagnut.com/blog/268/

80 http://picturefill.responsiveimages.org/

81 http://filamentgroup.com/lab/picturefill_2_a/

82 http://alistapart.com/article/dao

83 http://www.lukew.com/ff/archive.asp?tag&mobilefirst

84 http://adactio.com/journal/1716/

85 http://adactio.com/journal/4443/

86 http://timkadlec.com/2011/03/responsive-web-design-and-mobile-context/

87 http://globalmoxie.com/blog/mobile-web-responsive-design.shtml

88 http://blog.cloudfour.com/weekend-reading-responsive-web-design-and-mobile-context/

89 http://unstoppablerobotninja.com/entry/with-good-references/

90 http://unstoppablerobotninja.com/entry/toffee-nosed/

91 http://unstoppablerobotninja.com/entry/responsive-web-design-screens-and-shearing-layers/

INDEX

ABOUT A BOOK APART

We cover the emerging and essential topics in web design and development with style, clarity, and above all, brevity—because working designer-developers can't afford to waste time.

COLOPHON

The text is set in FF Yoga and its companion, FF Yoga Sans, both by Xavier Dupré. Headlines and cover are set in Titling Gothic by David Berlow.

MIX
Paper from
responsible sources
FSC® C103203
www.fsc.org

This book was printed in the United States using FSC certified Finch papers.